IMPROVING PERSONAL AND ORGANIZATIONAL
✓LEARNING,
✓ACCOUNTABILITY, AND
✓PERFORMANCE

An Eight-Step Systems Thinking Template for Success Based on the Fundamental Learning Cycle and the Behavioral Habits of Authentic Leadership

A Primer for Aspiring and New
Supervisors and Managers

With Easy-to-Learn
Useful Tools and Examples

H.F. (HERB) WIMMER

NEWMAN SPRINGS PUBLISHING
320 Broad Street
Red Bank, NJ 07701

First originally published by Newman Springs Publishing 2024

ISBN 979-8-89061-633-3 (Paperback)
ISBN 979-8-89061-635-7 (Hardcover)
ISBN 979-8-89061-634-0 (Digital)

Printed in the United States of America

Herb Wimmer's decades of leadership and mentorship experience shines through this impressively practical book, a wonderful guide for new and experienced managers alike.

Dr Paul Dodd, Associate Vice Chancellor, University of California, Davis

An insightful and adaptable eight step strategic game-plan from an experienced veteran of the American corporate trenches. A must read for aspiring young leaders.

John S. Hasbrook , Retired partner and VP, Sunwest Foods

No book will change your life but some can be a compelling inspiration for change. The best ones offer a roadmap to translate that inspiration into action. It is the action that can change lives; our own and others. This book offers both the inspiration and a functional road map for that change. I wish I had this book in my early career. It would have saved a lot of time, effort and learning the hard way. Thank you Herb.

Michael Hogan, M.S. Soil Scientist , Student, President (retired) Integrated Environmental Restoration Services, Inc.

As the Author states, people want agency. I want agency. I didn't realize what that fully meant, and I certainly did not have a written plan on how to get there. Which, as a lifelong planner, is more than a bit disconcerting. I wish I had read this book 25 years ago. We all rethink scenarios in our head on how we could have done something better. Well, how about we look at problems better. Get to the root of it, not the effect. Let's look at problems more systematically, look at possible roadblocks or offramps, and be prepared when they pop up, so we get it right the first run, or at minimum, improve our approach for the next problem. You may not know it now, but you want agency. Read this book to open that door.

Chris Lee, General Manager, Solano
County Water Agency

Best Primer on Organizational Learning and Effectiveness. This book blends adaptive management with systems thinking for a comprehensive yet approachable primer on how to align human intentions for effective group action. I have been mentored by the author for 20 years, putting these ideas into practice in the field of habitat restoration. Full of inspiring quotes and practical examples, this book provides you, the reader with the next best thing to Uncle Herb as your personal mentor. If you read just one book in the learning journey of your career, let this be the one.

Rich Marovich, Putah Creek Streamkeeper
(Emeritus), Solano County Water Agency

Relying on years of experience and research, Herb Wimmer introduces systems thinking skills and how they provide a fundamental element of effective leadership. This book is an outstanding primer for aspiring managers and a valuable refresher for the experienced manager, whether in the public or private sector.

Roland Sanford, Solano County Water
Agency General Manager, retired

As I was reading this book I had a recurring regret. I wished this had been available to me early in my career. I trained as an engineer and, then, a physician. When I assumed more senior roles, I had little leadership experience. It took me years of experience and hundreds of hours of study to arrive at the principles put forth here. Mr. Wimmer presents a path to leadership that is simple, practical, and effective. I highly recommend the book to anyone in a leadership position, but especially to those who are early in their career.

Robert Schultz, MD, Retired Physician-in-Chief,
Kaiser Permanente Medical Center Santa Rosa

For emerging leaders, understanding concepts like systems thinking and authentic leadership is paramount as they serve as the cornerstone upon which numerous other leadership principles are constructed. This book masterfully and simply presents these concepts in a highly digestible approach, empowering aspiring leaders with the confidence to embrace the journey of trial, success/failure, learning, and growth. It equips them to gain the essential experience needed to make meaningful contributions to their careers and the organizations they work with.

Charlie Thompson , President/CEO, Cagwin & Dorward

Things you would likely hear me saying!

We beget the kind of organizations we justly deserve

based on our leadership behaviors.

Unless you are learning faster than

your competition, the end is in sight.

We don't know

what we don't yet know.

If you always do what you always did,

You will always get what you always got.

If you want to get what you never got,

You have to do what you never did.

Who Will Do What By When, Exactly?

Adult learning is considered a "very hard" skill. It takes courage, persistence, honesty, humility, tact, and compassion. These are the human interaction skills of accomplished leaders. These behaviors set the tone for a culture of learning or not.

We want to be learners, not knowers!

Facts are our friends! Let's find 'em and use 'em!

One of the interesting things about poor judgment is we do not know we have it—blessing or curse?

Don't worry people aren't listening to you,
worry they are watching you
and taking their cues from what they see in your behaviors,
perhaps when you are not at your best.

DEDICATION

I dedicate this book to my lovely wife of almost six decades, Christine Ann Unger Wimmer, and to our lovely, talented, and successful daughters, Nancy Ann Wimmer Veatch and Janice Lynn Wimmer Corbett (RIP). Our daughters have been a source of inspiration and learning for me on many levels. My life would be meaningless if I could not share it with Christine. Nothing I have ever accomplished would have been possible without her. She has stood by me with sensitive, caring, intelligent guidance and gentle assistance with every step, from our teen years to this moment.

CONTENTS

———— ⌒✺⌒ ————

PREFACE

Just how effective are you, really? How effective is your organization? What processes do you rely on, and what routine behaviors do you practice individually and collectively that bring about reliable and blossoming success? What new behaviors can you learn and practice now to get on a steady path of increasing success?

This book is intended to help. It will be easy to digest and useful, especially since it provides tools and some actual working examples. Based on systems thinking, it ties mental models, brain styles, cultural habits, systemic processes, and especially authentic leadership behaviors together in an eight-step template for moving ever more effectively toward your desired results.

I will describe these elements in relatively brief simple terms. I have included a supplemental chapter on Systems Thinking (chapter 12) for those who want to go deeper to know more about the source of these ideas. I highly recommend you choose to read that first. I also list some additional resources in the bibliography, that way you can skim my materials that you may be comfortable with or care less about, and you can go deeper to other listed resources to get more detail, theory, applications, etc. With the internet, it is so easy to look things up; you can do that if you run across processes or terms that you are not familiar with. Thus, I will not spend much time and space repeating things you likely already know or could easily look up.

I use the term Mental Models to express the idea that we each have ways of thinking patterned in our brains by our accumulated experiential learning. These can and are usually quite helpful, but they can also be like a ball and chain if we don't also explore other alternative ways of thinking. We will be dancing with the challenge of whether we hold mental models or if our mental models hold us for the rest of this book.

We don't know what we don't yet know.

By now you are wondering what I mean by brain styles. For me, that term refers to the fact that we each have our own way of relating to the world, our own way of thinking, and our own mental models for how the world works. For example, much has been written about left brain–right brain thinking and other brain-style systems.

While too simple and not perfect for our use, brain styles are one highly simplified idea that can nevertheless be powerful in opening the door to better understanding of ourselves relative to others. I will be saying more about this and other brain-style frameworks later. I think considering some of the various brain styles can be a fruitful path toward understanding how individuals and teams struggle or succeed. You have a dominant way of thinking. Do you know what your brain style is and how it affects you and those around you? Read on. Change is the path to ever higher levels of performance. Stasis is the path to nowhere.

How do you react to needed or desired changes identified by you versus changes that emerge from outside yourself?

I love change when I get to change you.
When you try to change me,
I don't like it as much.

Notice I use the word *performance*. I prefer this word to the currently popular word *execution*, which seems more remote, negative, and less descriptive of what needs to actually happen. High performance comes from behaviors, your behaviors, and the well-intended, organized, and focused aggregate behaviors of those around you, pure and simple.

Be the change, you want
to see in the world.
—Mahatma Gandhi

New destinations call for new maps.

I hope you learn and enjoy the book. I hope it brings you to new higher levels of learning, accountability, and the resultant personal and organizational behaviors that bring consistent high performance!

H. F. "Herb" Wimmer
Winters, CA

I hope someday my tombstone says,
"He helped others find success!"

ACKNOWLEDGMENTS

In my early years in an R&D work culture, I learned the critical value of specific plans. And I learned the value of being accountable for both our efforts and our results using quality measurement processes. This is the key to learning and development of ideas, processes, products, and organizational capacity. I know how hard that is to do well and how very, very important it is. It takes humility and persistent discipline.

Along the way, I have worked with and for many extremely talented and highly educated individuals who contributed to my current state of thinking. Thus, I am not the creator of any of the ideas expressed here. I could name many, but then certainly, I would have left many out, so I choose to honor them by sharing what I learned from them.

I have learned and adapted ideas that I think support the central mission of learning, accountability, and performance. These "borrowed" ideas came out of minds much more capable than mine. I assembled them into a process that I know works well and will be most useful to you. The good ideas shared here really belong to others; the errors or misjudgments are solely my own.

About three decades ago, I was introduced to systems thinking as a more formal way of thinking and behaving. Life has not been the same since. I found a whole new outlook and passion for how to view the world and my role in it.

After retiring in 2000 from Chevron, I spent the next twenty years working as a one-man teacher and coach of systems thinking, process improvement, and mostly leadership development. My hands-on learning comes from my years as an individual contributor, team leader, supervisor, manager of a large business unit, and then later teaching and coaching individuals, teams, and leaders in a number of public agencies and businesses.

For eleven years, till the pandemic arrived, I had the privilege of teaching a survey course on systems thinking at UC Davis in their staff leadership development series. I called it Systems Thinking: The Human Side of Systems. I learned more researching, writing, and leading that class than I ever did any other way. That experience tied all my ideas together into a useful process—the core of this book.

I feel that at this point in my journey, I need to share what I have learned with others who are on a quest for personal and organizational improvement. I wish you much luck on your quest. I hope this book is part of that effort and a useful foundation for your future success.

***Luck seems to come to those most
capable and best prepared.***

Do you want to improve personal and organizational learning, accountability, and performance? Here is your guide!

CHAPTER 1

——— ✺ ———

I Am an Authentic Process Leader, I Teach and Lead by Example!

Chapter Summary

This chapter provides a general orientation to what is to follow, and it describes the leadership behaviors and culture needed to build persistent and sustainable leadership habits for learning, accountability, and high performance. The ideas here and the eight-step process can change your career and your life. It can bring you to new insights about yourself, about leading others, and how you can move to create sustainable and blossoming value and a high-performance culture that promotes individual and organizational learning, accountability, and high performance.

You will notice this book has a number of seemingly redundant sections. That is quite intentional. Just go with the flow and enjoy the apparent repeats that are used as a way to reinforce concepts. Each time, the repeated next idea is at a deeper and thus higher and richer level of understanding (e.g., the process of learning for an individual vs. for a

1

group), so please just digest the steps in order when they seem redundant and look for the repeating and ever-enriching patterns. Each time the idea is repeated, I hope you will view it more thoughtfully and thus value it more.

As an individual contributor or a leader at some level, we each need to "own" the systems we create, refine, are working in, and tolerate. In fact, you might eventually come to believe we fully justly deserve the systems we have created or live with, good or poor. We are responsible for our own behaviors, work processes, work product, and yes, our current systems. And we are frequently part of teams sharing responsibilities or even being responsible for the work of others. What a complex set of systems!

> *What is the world our children deserve?*
> *—Nelson Mandela*

As an organizational leader at some level (we are all leaders in that we set examples of behavior observed, appreciated, and replicated, or perhaps despised and avoided by others), I have learned not to worry that others are not listening to me. I know that they are watching and judging me and my behaviors and being positively or negatively reinforced by what they see. I am reminded of the quote of one of my early mentors:

> *The flowers grow best in the*
> *shadow of the master*
> *—Marion "Tubby" Snodgrass*

Think about the impact of the behavior of our leaders on us and everything we do. Official leader or not, think of how your behaviors affect all those around you, for better or worse, no matter your intentions. Think about when important people in your life are grumpy or happy. What effect does that have on you? What about when you choose to be happy or grumpy? Happy or grumpy is always a choice. What effect does that have on others? What is the pattern of behavior you are known for? Can you actually be the person you would really like to work with?

I use and repeat the term *behaviors* frequently. Behaviors are what we actually do, not just what we think about, hold firm opinions about, or ideas we share with others. Think about it, behaviors are what actually make things happen. Skills, processes, worldviews, mental models, and mindsets are important, and other writers place primary emphasis on these. I place my bets on actual behaviors. What are the behavioral habits leading to success?

As more and more people follow your lead and practice the behaviors of learning and accountability, the capacity and thus performance of the entire organization rises. A rising tide lifts all boats. Eventually, as new people join you, they will want to fit in. They will quickly align with the high-performance culture as being "the way things are done here." Conversely, if this is a dysfunctional culture, they will join you there too! We get what we deserve! Take steps to steadily move the culture in a positive direction. This is the process of building a highly effective learning/accountability/performance culture.

My intention is to help you build a repertoire of effective routine leadership behaviors in a consistently applied eight-step system that leads to success based on demonstrated principles, systems thinking processes, mental models, brain styles, culture, and effective habits. So look for that difference throughout the book. I like the phrase "you are what you repeatedly do." No matter what self-image dominates your mind, the world only experiences you as your actual behaviors.

You have a well-earned reputation. Do you really know what it is? Is it the one you really deserve or want to have? Is it the one you will need to influence others to higher levels of performance by them actually emulating your behaviors? How would you actually get that reputation? What would that set of leadership behaviors look like?

Don't worry they aren't listening; they are watching!

Learning and accountability are capacities that can be expanded with the proper focus. They are the individual and collective behaviors practiced with discipline that create more effective performance. They are a way of thinking and a way of being. No matter our level of competency, we can always learn, improve, and accept more responsibility and continue to refine these behaviors to ever higher levels of performance by persistently challenging ourselves. No matter how far west you are, you can always go farther west.

The supplemental chapter will be helpful if you are curious about the core ideas that brought me to build the eight-step system template. I encourage you to take a look at chapter 12 now or after you digest the rest of the book.

I think if you do, you will then want to study more about systems thinking as a next step on your learning journey.

We all have strong points and weak points. While our strong points may carry us far, our weak points are the things holding us back from even greater success, no matter how you define it. We need to be using our strong points to cure our weak points. If enough people think you are a poor leader, face it, you are a poor leader no matter what you think! If others try to avoid you due to your behavior, think of the pool of available talent, ideas, and cooperation that is not available to you.

Be mindful of what you practice as you steadily become better at it; if it is actually detrimental, you are gradually getting worse! Higher performance comes by paying attention to and practicing what is most needed, not what is most familiar or comfortable.

> *Marines—Not practice what you preach*
> *preach what you practice*
> *(And improve on both as you go)*
> *—Unknown*

Psychologists distinguish between "self-oriented perfectionism," in which people put pressure on themselves to perform flawlessly, and "other oriented perfectionism," in which people hold their colleagues to the highest of standards while tending to ignore failings in their own performance. Which are you?

No one learns more than the teacher. So by learning and mastering this way of thinking, being, and behaving, you will begin teaching these ideas to others. Use your own new behaviors as examples as you become increasingly effective yourself. Hold yourself to a very high standard; be more forgiving of others.

First, master the behaviors yourself till they become your habits. Drive yourself to become more aware of your learning and more accountable as the first acid test of this approach. Don't expect others to do what you can't do.

Digest these mental models, practice the cultural habits, follow the outlined eight-step systems thinking process and patterns of behavior till they become cultural habits that lead to success. My years of work in this field tell me you have to practice something at least sixty-six times for it to become your way of doing and being. Smile. That may seem too simple, but I do think it is largely correct.

Don't think this is a short-term approach. If you want better outcomes, continually practice, refine, master, lead, teach, and model these behaviors in how you personally work, and eventually, require nothing less in yourself and eventually from those you lead or influence.

We want the new way to become "the way things are done here" and inspire others by our example and personal success. Be the person others look to for high performance based on your track record of smart and effective leadership behaviors that show the way for others. Don't worry people aren't listening to you; worry they are watching you and taking their cues from what they see in your behaviors, perhaps when you are not at your best.

While this book is about improving learning, accountability, and performance in organizations, we tend to think changes are all needed in *others*. This book is primarily about improving learning, accountability, and performance for *ourselves* in our own work, with the goal of then leading and teaching others, mostly by the example of our behavior. Let's focus on the only part of the world we can actually control.

Learning, accountability, and timely effective performance are something we all want for ourselves and need to master to lead successful organizations. Let's be honest, we really focus on and like learning, accountability, and great performance most when we think those words describe us. We sometimes observe and acknowledge it in others and organizations.

We appreciate this when others meet our needs and expectations without our needing to pester them. We also most quickly and easily recognize a lack of accountability and performance in others when it delays or blocks our own path to success or fulfillment. What about ourselves? Are we someone else's roadblock? Do we know? Do we attempt to find out? How often?

If we are truly honest with ourselves, we know that we subtly find ways to minimize or avoid accountability (or fool ourselves at least) for our own performance. Oh, not consciously, just subconsciously...and well!

> ***Damn it! Do what I say, not what I do!***
> ***—Herb Wimmer Sr.***

Ask yourself, why do young children approach learning with wonder and adults approach learning (being openly vulnerable and being forthcoming about less-than-stellar performance) with hesitancy and some level of fear?

Watch a toddler learning to walk or climb their first stairs. They are persistent. They don't care who is watching; in fact, they like to be encouraged while trying. When they fail, they just laugh and try again. They keep trying new approaches to master the challenge. Adults want to learn in private. We don't want to publicly air our lack of knowledge, abilities, or failings.

We have egos to protect, frequently at the expense of our own advancement in knowledge and capability. Most of us pretend to know things we do not in order to not have to admit to others and perhaps not even to ourselves that we do not know.

Why don't we like being called on when we fail to meet objectives? Why are we reluctant to report our own lack of understanding and failings? Why are we as individuals so blind to taking serious stock of our own learning, accountability, and performance? We all know that acknowledging a deficit is the first step to overcoming it.

Take a moment and reflect on this more. Are you as accountable personally as you expect others to be? Really? Can you tell yourself the truth, the real hard truth? Are your critics actually correct? Perhaps just a little? You might long to improve accountability in others. The sure path is to become highly accountable in your own work behaviors and show the way by your behaviors. Don't expect others to do what you can't do.

The world is changed by your
example, not by your opinion.
—Paulo Coelho

Figure 1 gives some more perspective on all this focus on behaviors. In my view, the most important person in the mix is you and how you conduct yourself. Even if you are not in some official position of authority at the moment, your behaviors affect your work and everyone around you. You react to your environment, and all those that experience your behaviors do as well. Are you getting the reaction you want or need?

Sometimes in leadership classes, I hear people say, "My boss does not behave this way, so why should I?" So I guess if your boss is a jerk, you should try to emulate them? If your boss fails to lead effectively, should you follow their lead? That's a great plan! Good luck to you!

Given the right mindset, having a poor leader as a boss for a while can be a valuable education. Although this book is not about applied behavioral sciences, I heartily suggest you find some time to study up on that subject. I recommend *Bringing Out the Best in People* by Aubrey Daniels.

> *We beget the kind of organizations*
> *we deserve based on our*
> *leadership behaviors.*
> *—Unknown*

The very idea of learning and accountability calls for discipline—discipline in thinking and discipline in behavior, discipline in me, yes, ME. Consistent performance discipline is hard, damn hard. It calls for consistent and systematic application of specific high-value patterns of behavior to ensure we do exactly what we say we will do, by when, and in advance to say clearly what we will do so others have rational expectations of us.

Figure 1

Why all this Focus on Behaviors ?

Behavior is anything a person says or does [good or bad] AND it is
  also what a person does not say or do [sitting quietly is also a behavior]

<u>Four Major Ideas About Behavior to Remember</u> :

1) Your behavior as a leader directly affects everyone around you
    [if you think it doesn't , try disappearing for a few days and see what happens]

2) Everyone's behavior is a response to the environment in which it occurs
    [organizations are perfectly tuned to get what they get , for better or worse]

3) Your behavior directly affects your and your organizations success
    [the better you understand the effects of your behavior , separating them
      from your intentions the better you can influence success]

4) You can learn powerful tools for optimizing your leadership behaviors
    and the performance of everyone around you.
      [Applied Behavioral Science is the study of what people do and why]

We know what happens when others aren't accountable for their actions. We get frustrated when others are vague about what they plan to do and don't perform as we expect. We may not be thinking much about our own learning, accountability, and performance.

How are our actual performance actions (behaviors) perceived by others? How does that affect our reputation, our own success, and eventually the success of everyone around us? Personal accountability is the key and the core of this book. We always want to make clear who will do exactly what by when. And then actually DO IT.

Every organization serves two masters: its customers and its bottom line. Even nonprofits and all volunteer organizations have to meet the same tests of efficacy or risk decline. It takes the discipline of the leadership to ensure these are both being satisfied to survive and thrive.

I recently read a passage in *BusinessWeek* magazine stating, "Accountability, that means having a leader who is willing to own their mistakes" and "We don't expect leaders to be perfect, but we expect them to have the humility to admit they are fallible and that goes a long way to retaining the trust of the team." No matter your official position, you are a leader by example, and you can show that by being open and humble enough to be working on your own weaknesses.

> *The price of knowledge is the sum*
> *of all your fears about learning.*
> *—Fred Kofman*

We tend to judge ourselves by our good intentions, and we want to be judged by others for our good intentions, but we tend to judge others mostly by their behaviors and results. Read that last sentence again. Think of some examples from your life that confirm that reality. Others may have great intentions, which, of course, are usually hidden from us, but we are relying on their results, damn it! When we fail to deliver as promised, we know all the "reasons" for our lack of delivery. When someone else fails to deliver as promised, we frequently hear all the reasons for the lapse as "excuses," not reasons.

We sometimes consider the "excuses" of others when they fail to deliver as personality flaws or traits rather than as revelation and recognition of the obstacles they actually faced. Yet we consider the obstacles we faced as acceptable "reasons" for our failure. I highly recommend you look up "Fundamental Attribution Error" right now for a deeper explanation of this phenomenon if you are not familiar with it. You can read about it in *The Leadership Equation* by Lee and Norma Barr, PhD. There will also be much to easily digest about this on the internet. Understanding this can fundamentally change how we think about ourselves and others and our lives on many levels. Yes, stop and look that up now. It is formative to the thinking and behaviors of quality leadership.

This basic psychology concept is very important for individuals and especially leaders to understand. We preach accountability and complain when it is absent. Truly high-performance leaders chart the course by starting with themselves. They lead, teach, and coach by example. They show others by their behavior what success looks like.

> *Teach the Gospel at all times.*
> *When necessary, use words.*
> *—Saint Francis of Assisi*

The following early chapters each present specific behavioral steps that will be accumulated and then put to use when we bring this all together in the later chapters. Each is valuable in its own right. You may be familiar with some or all of them. I encourage you to read about them here again step by step as the application or context may be different for this use from your memory or experience.

The eight steps are many more times powerful when combined into a comprehensive systematic routine behavioral model for learning, accountability, and performance. That is synergy. Milk is good, cookies are good, milk and cookies are really, really good—ahhhh! Synergy!

There is really nothing new here. Think about it, in human systems, fundamentally, there is nothing new under the sun. I have accumulated these ideas from my own career work, study, and prior experiences. I have knit them together into this eight-step systems thinking process that makes them highly effective in building learning, accountability, and performance. But they are not mine; they are as old as mankind.

W. Edwards Deming, the famous guru of high performance and the quality movement that revolutionized the world of manufacturing and product quality in the 1980s, spoke of a conundrum that plagued him. He wondered why organizations focused so much more attention on getting the best people, yet focused much too little attention on building great processes—the very routine high-quality processes and systems critical for high performance.

> *You do not have to change—*
> *survival is not mandatory!*
> *—W. Edwards Deming*

When outcomes are measured, we give too much credit or blame to individuals and too little credit or blame to our underlying process systems. You can read more about this in *Learning Organizations: Developing Cultures for Tomorrow's Workplace* by Fred Kofman et al. Smart leaders build and then rigorously manage robust quality routine systemic processes so that dedicated, hardworking people can practice them well and be successful.

I know you will already be familiar with most of these eight steps. They are not new inventions. They may all be boringly familiar to you. Don't reject or ignore them till you give the *whole system* a chance! The prize is to assemble and use them in powerful routine patterns of behavior, a systems thinking approach of process behaviors. When practiced together consistently as behavioral habits, they raise the bar of learning, accountability, and performance for you and your organization. The key is consistent and systematic repetitious application of the eight-step process to the challenges we face.

Perhaps when things are going haywire, you have heard people say, "We have to think about what we are doing." I know they have that backward. I have learned it should be "We have to do something about what we are thinking." Most everything in the world is created in the mind first. A new house, a new process, a new product, etc. If you can't think it, you certainly can't do it. So think about what is missing from your thinking before you start acting.

Don't be afraid to give up the
good to go for the great.
— John D. Rockefeller

This book relies on old standby ideas and focused new ways of patterned thinking that use a consistent approach to meeting new challenges. I will introduce this term here and use this term many times again: Consistent And Systematic Application (CASA). Watch for this mantra as it is key to repetition of success-driving behaviors.

One of the tools you can learn to use to identify the deep cause of some system or organizational problem is called the Five Whys. It is in common use across the world by smart systems thinking leaders to find root causes. Most of us fail to use it when the problem is right in front of us. Perhaps the problem is too familiar for us to be clearheaded and objective when thinking about it.

Perhaps we are blind to our own limited thinking about our challenges. In order to be most effective, we need to be sure we are actually working on the root cause of the problem. Problems create second-order spin-off effects that masquerade as the core problem.

You have experienced this with others when they tell you of the problems they are facing, and when you look at the problem, the solutions seem so simple to you. You can see through their story and pick out the core issue to be solved, yet when you yourself are faced with a problem, you usually can't easily see the root cause while others point out things that would make it easier to solve.

The Five Whys is a very useful tool mastered and in use by systems thinkers all over the world. I have included here just two examples that I have used in classes about systems thinking. I urge you to study these two and ask yourself when will you start to use this valuable tool. You want to be sure you are working on the root cause of the problem, not just its external manifestations.

The Five Whys are used to reveal the root causes of our problem. It is a diagnostic tool, not a solution tool. It takes the leadership behavior of discipline to understand the root of the problem before we unleash a rush of resources to solve the problem. So we use this tool first, and once we have a good understanding of the underlying drivers of our challenge, then we focus on how to solve the root issue.

Five Whys Example One
Systems Thinking or Stinking?: *Adapted from an article in the* San Francisco Chronicle, *February 28, 2000*

> THE FIRST WHY. *This last summer, as the San Francisco Giants were streaming toward winning the World Series, there was a noticeable stench surrounding their home field, AT&T Park. During past baseball seasons, fans continually complained of the low-tide stink.*
>
> THE SECOND WHY. *The Giants' ballyard hugs the San Francisco Bay. During low tide, as the bay water ebbs and microscopic organisms in the mud are exposed to air and rapidly begin to decay, a rotten smell appears. The city has already spent $100 million over the past five years to upgrade its sewer system and sewage plants. There is a lot of momen-*

tum among the citizens and in the agencies that are seeking solutions.

THE THIRD WHY. The City of San Francisco is stocking up on a $14-million three-year supply of highly concentrated sodium hypochlorite—better known as bleach—to act as an odor eater and to disinfect the city's treated water before it is dumped into the SF Bay. It will also be used to sanitize drinking water. This means nearly nine million pounds of bleach will either be poured down city drains or into the drinking water supply every year. However, the sulfur-like scent wasn't the result of the ways of the sea.

THE FOURTH WHY. In the past few decades, many of us have come to believe we need to conserve water in order to be responsible stewards of our natural resources. Like almost every other city in the US, San Francisco has been educating citizens and mandating the switch to low-flow toilets. They started a taxpayer-funded rebate program to help locals upgrade. Shortly thereafter, city engineers started noticing sewer backups. Since then, the city has had to spend $100 million in large measures to combat the problem caused by the low-flow units.

THE FIFTH WHY. Skimping on toilet water has resulted in more sludge backing up inside the sewer pipes, says the Public Utilities Commission. That has created the rotten-egg stench near AT&T Park and elsewhere, especially during the dry summer months. Unfortunately, to avoid sewer back-ups, many have started flushing multiple times to mitigate potential backups. How's that for water conservation logic?

Questions: *What was the original mindset? Do you think anyone carefully studied the potential unintended consequences of the original plan so that they could be mitigated? Do you have a process for evaluating unintended consequences in your decision-making process?*

Five Why's Example Two
The Invasive Spotted Knapweed
Adapted from an article in Canadian Field Naturalist, May 2001

THE FIRST WHY. This noxious weed is a European invader that, over the last hundred years, has spread throughout the pastures and rangeland of western North America. It often outcompetes native species. It landed on the West Coast in the 1890s, probably carried in a shipment of alfalfa seed or in soil used as ballast.

THE SECOND WHY. To combat it, agricultural agencies began to introduce a type of insect called a Gall Fly of the genus Urophora in the 1970s. The flies' larvae build galls within the flower buds and steal some of the plant's energy, leading to a reduction in the number of seeds that develop. This was an attempt to slow the rate of invasion.

THE THIRD WHY. Unfortunately, it turns out that the deer mouse views these larvae as yummy snacks and, while foraging for them, may accidentally ingest whole knapweed seeds. Since the seeds can survive passage through the mouse's digestive system, the little mammal may contribute to the knapweeds' dispersal.

THE FOURTH WHY. Seeds may travel even farther if an owl catches the mouse and then, at the end of its meal, regurgitates the seeds along with the undigested bones (this is what owls do).

THE FIFTH WHY. The introduction of Gall Flies provides one more example of an important fact. Once introduced, species become part of the larger ecological web with possibly unforeseen consequences. Now we may be faced with some other unintended

*consequence of the Gall Fly, which we will
learn about eventually.*

Questions:
*What was the original mindset? Could this outcome have
been avoided? How?*

Before you go off trying to solve some problem or capture some opportunity, take some careful time to challenge your thinking about what the core issue really is. Try to solve the root problem, not the symptom.

Ask the five whys. Get clear on exactly what the issue is before you start to work toward a goal. What would success look like? Are we sure we are working on the core drivers of poor performance? Now, let's move on to more about individual and group learning.

> **We see the world, not as it is,
> but as we are conditioned to see it.**
> **—Stephen R. Covey**

Stepping out to make improvements in ourselves or our organizations can drive us to search for and adopt a "program" to make it all happen. Beware of "programs." By definition, programs end. We want embedded continuous process learning, accountability, and performance. We want this to be the way we do things here, routine behaviors that are embedded in our way of thinking, period, not something we just try for a while. This comes from inside us, from our own internal learning and new behaviors, not some program developed by others. We want to become different, not just try on some shiny new coat to see if it fits.

What if I underpromised and overdelivered every time? What if I was known for solving problems that did not just come back again?

> **If it is not in you, it can't
> come out of you.**

Chapter Summary

Real progress in developing improved individual or collective learning, accountability, and performance comes from the very hard work of disciplined authentic leadership behaviors based on understanding others and human nature.

CHAPTER 2

—— ❧ ——

PDCA: A Mental Model for How Individuals Learn

Chapter Summary

This chapter builds the basic foundation of understanding for the eight-step template, which will come in chapter 5. It describes the fundamental learning cycle in detail for an individual and how it is used to improve ourselves and our processes over time.

Perhaps you have seen this before?

Plan—Do—Check—Adjust = PDCA

This is the fundamental learning cycle underlying most applications of systems thinking, learning, process improvement, adaptive management, capacity building, and high performance. There are many alternative versions going back many decades, but they are all quite similar, varying mostly in word choice. Most models in use today have more than four steps, yet contain the four critical steps of **PDCA.** Please review figure 2 before proceeding.

The key is performing the critical steps and maintaining the cyclical nature of the process, not the number of steps used to describe it. The adjust step is actually the most important as it refers to adjusting your next plan from what you learned from implementing the last plan, thus making a cycle. This is very important. Less-effective problem-solving or planning tools are linear in nature, such as A then B then C then D, then stop. The critical missing element is the feedback loop of checking and adjusting so critical to continuous process improvement from the learning provided by a circular model.

While I did not actually recognize it then, I first studied systems thinking in this cyclical way in an excellent little book called *The Universal Traveler* by Don Koberg and Jim Bagnall in college in the early seventies. This book was my first exposure to using simple diagrams to understand complex ideas. In industry, we were using systems thinking and images to promote better learning and performance in the Total Quality Management movement in the early 1980s.

Figure 2

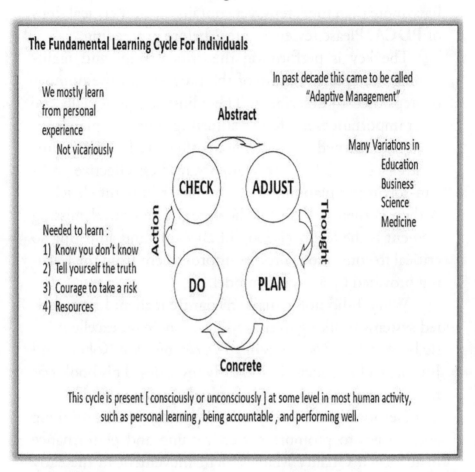

The Fundamental Learning Cycle For Individuals

We mostly learn from personal experience
Not vicariously

In past decade this came to be called "Adaptive Management"

Abstract

Many Variations in
Education
Business
Science
Medicine

CHECK   ADJUST

Action   Thought

Needed to learn :
1) Know you don't know
2) Tell yourself the truth
3) Courage to take a risk
4) Resources

DO   PLAN

Concrete

This cycle is present [consciously or unconsciously] at some level in most human activity, such as personal learning , being accountable , and performing well.

In the early 1990s, I discovered this powerful way of sharing ideas again in a book called *The Organizational Learning Cycle* by Nancy Dixon. It took much too long for me to fully appreciate its value. This simple graphic cycle is so simple that it is easy to ignore, yet is the key to organizational learning, accountability, and performance.

The **PDCA** chart shows the circular nature of the process flow, which is critical. Planning and doing are concrete activities. Checking and adjusting are more abstract. Doing and checking are action-like, while adjusting and planning are more driven by deeper thinking.

This is the fundamental cycle that is used extensively across the world. In order to be ready to learn, you have to

1) know you don't know,
2) tell yourself the truth,
3) have the courage to take an ego risk of trying something new, and
4) align resources and then act.

Humans mostly learn from experience. We rarely learn by listening to the stories of others. This is why it is so important to pursue learning experiences within a logical framework with a clear understanding how learning occurs. We need a process model that we can follow to completion every time.

In my early line manager career in a Fortune 50 corporation, I was too busy trying to "manage" and control outcomes in an old-style command-and-control linear way to fully understand systems thinking's power to bring about increasingly higher levels of high-quality performance based on learning and accountability.

I was too focused on just getting the work done to notice that I needed to focus as much or more on if or how the systems we relied on could actually produce the results we wanted. Think about this in terms of your own struggles. This is a critical question. What is the system behind the work? If your system does not actually have the capacity to produce the required output, no amount of pushing will make it so.

> *Smart leaders work ON the system.*
> *Less smart managers*
> *work IN the system.*

A more detailed model of **PDCA** for organizations can be found in an excellent book called *The Fifth Discipline Fieldbook* by Peter Senge et al. Their model called for Joint Planning, Coordinated Action, Public Reflection, and Shared Meaning, moving from how one person might use this to how a group might use it. This is another version of **PDCA** with application beyond one person. We will cover this critical area later in chapter 3. There are many other versions of this cycle using different names for the same basic cyclical activities. No matter what you call them, you need all four to build system capacity for sustained success.

This may seem familiar to you for another reason. It is based on the "scientific method" used across the last several hundred years across the education system across the planet. Its adoption and broad application changed life on our planet in dramatic ways. You studied this in school.

The scientific method seeks resolution to a problem or to grasp some understanding or opportunity. It forms a hypothesis about how to succeed, tests the hypothesis by trying something while holding other factors steady, measures the results, draws conclusions, and then applies those to the next trial. This learning process is based on gradual improvement, gradually bringing us closer to our goal. I have heard this well described as successive approximations to the goal.

> *It is not the most intellectual of the*
> *species that survives; it is not the*
> *strongest that survives; but the species*
> *that survives is the one that is able best*
> *to adapt and adjust to the changing*
> *environment in which it finds itself.*
> —*Charles Darwin, Origin of Species*

A quick lookup online will show this circular process improvement model in very limited use in the late 1940s all the way to relatively widespread use today. In the early years, it was more theoretical, scientific, about large-scale manufacturing process improvement, and applied initially most effectively in post-WWII industrial Japan.

PDCA played a large part in the theory and teachings of the "quality movement "in the US in the 1980s. The big advantage of the cycle is that feedback for improvement is built-in. Linear project management and problem-solving tools do not have this feature so critical to learning and thus continuous process improvement.

In the past two decades, the **PDCA** model has found new currency in the medical, military, research, business, and environmental worlds recently as "Adaptive Management." I share this history so you know it has been around a long while and is in use by many in education, industry, and public agencies today.

PDCA sounds too simple to be valuable. Now, I realize I was exposed to this so many years ago and only in the past twenty-five years gained enough personal wisdom from my life experiences as a line manager to capitalize on the prize of understanding and relying on it. You can easily look up the history or dive deeper into the texts listed here or elsewhere for many diverse applications, so let's move on to how you might find it useful.

PDCA is a foundational process in learning, account-ability, and performance. Once fully understood, one can look back on prior poor performances and see evidence of broken **PDCA** cycles where one of the steps was missing. All four steps are needed to ensure learning, accountability, and performance. If one or more steps are missing, there will be no improvement.

> *An organization's ability to learn,*
> *and translate that learning into*
> *action rapidly, is the ultimate*
> *competitive advantage.*
> —*Jack Welch*

Going Deeper with the Individual Learning Cycle

PDCA

My goal is to keep this simple, yet the **PDCA** model and behaviors have multiple layers to consider and benefit from. This seemingly simple model can be used in many ways to improve performance in complex systems. Here we will build it up one layer at a time, till the model is complete and can be applied. Let's walk around the circle, building the **PDCA** cycle one step at a time.

Unfortunately, careful thinking is rare when facing some new challenge. We tend to take comfort in our unconscious intuitive drive for action. This can be very reinforcing and wrong. Careful thinking is a slower process of conscious analysis and reasoning before making any PLANS. I urge you to study more about this in *Make It Stick* by Peter C. Brown et al.

It is very important to note, this first pass is for the learning cycle for one person alone, the individual learning cycle. Later in the next chapter, we will build the same **PDCA** cycle when more than one brain is involved. Each application has important learnings for leaders.

P = PLAN

Everything human made in the world is created in the mind first. Your car, soda pop, TV, iPhone, house, freeway, ham sandwich, new back fence, TV ads, new products, new services, etc., were all conceived in someone's mind and then assembled in the world. While we may not think we are planning much to make a sandwich or other familiar things, planning is always occurring.

The buildings you live and work in were assembled from plans, materials, and construction processes. Projects, results, and even organizations come to be as a result of planning. Planning is the first and frequently subconscious step to bring about a result.

Poor planning leads to poor outcomes. If we are smart enough to analyze and recognize them, poor outcomes reveal the missing links of learning from our failures. Failing to fully understand the nature of the challenge at hand is too frequently familiar to most of us. If you can't fully define the problem at the start, any solutions will only be working on the part of the problem you could define, isolate, and understand. The rest of the challenge lies hidden, lurking, goes unaddressed, and usually returns.

On the other hand, we never have perfect information or time to figure out all the many aspects of a situation. The 80–20 concept is a useful guide. If you are not familiar with the 80–20 rule, look it up before going further. Yes, go look it up! Look for the "Pareto Principle."

> ### *The easy way out usually leads back in.*
> ### *—Peter Senge*

In problem-solving, explore what is needed, see what resources you can count on, choose the best alternatives, consider risks, and make a PLAN. Write it down. A PLAN in your head is not really a reliable PLAN. If you doubt this, study memory processes (look up "rates of forgetting"), then come back and join those who have learned that unless the PLAN is written down, it is not really a PLAN, it is more of a vague intention. Expect vague results!

In the next step, actually follow the PLAN exactly. So easy! Just actually follow the PLAN to the letter. I like the old saying, "Plan the work and work the plan." A written PLAN has value too for future reference. If PLANs are only in our heads, we have no accurate accumulation of data months later for what actually worked and what didn't and why.

We assume what actually happened was what we planned. It may have been what we intended, but we did not get there by following our PLAN since we did not really have a PLAN. We miss the chance to learn from the experience. We paid for it, why miss it?

Memories are very unreliable records of unwritten intentions (so-called NOPLANs). We have no way to analyze trends or build data toward better understanding for our next attempt from NOPLANs. Get in the habit of creating written PLANs for important things and, in fact, for many things.

Frequently, people write process manuals and instructions. This is the PLAN to be followed for given situations. We do this to help keep us on track to get things done correctly and completely. We usually do this in response to prior failures. These well-intentioned efforts frequently end up holding down dusty bookcases but are not actually followed as they are perceived as being too complex and burdensome to follow.

They are complex since many try to accommodate most any eventuality. An effective PLAN must be simple enough to remember and detailed enough to cover the critical challenges and know if we arrived at our intended destination or someplace else. In coming chapters, I will lay out a process to do this. The key is building an adaptive plan.

This book is dedicated to the disciplined CASA approach of **PDCA**. We want to steadily move toward data/fact-driven processes and PLANs. Well-documented facts are powerful. Opinions are much less reliable and thus less valuable about what actually works and what doesn't.

Opinions and memories are unreliable; documented facts are not. Facts come from measuring things. Memory is flawed and malleable. If you doubt this, go look it up now. Write things down. Document PLANs and subsequent process improvements to them over time, with data measured along the way.

> *He who fails to plan is planning to fail.*
> *—Winston Churchill*

Written PLANS form the beginning of all quality process-improvement cycles. History is littered with examples where known facts and good processes have even been written down and later forgotten or ignored, and lessons had to be learned over and over again, painfully.

Think of the 1986 NASA *Challenger* spacecraft disaster, for example, a terrible disaster in a world of excellent PLANS not followed due to lack of discipline. An unwritten PLAN is able to be interpreted by many in whatever way they choose at any point in time, so everyone may be well intentioned and yet moving in clearly different directions in their own interpretation of the same unwritten PLAN. It is hard enough to follow a good written PLAN given the frailty of our language, but it is much better than a NOPLAN.

> *If you aim at nothing, you*
> *will hit it every time.*
> *—Zig Ziglar*

The PLAN phase is where our mission, vision, values, and strategy for this effort are clarified. If you don't know where you want to be, then anywhere is good. If you can't point to where you want to go, you will never know if you've arrived. This leads to ceaseless striving for vague, undefined outcomes and thus low efficiency for individuals and especially for groups. Written PLANs do not have to be fancy; they just need to have clearly stated missions, visions, values, strategies, tactics, and measures fixed in time, space, resource use, people, and with clear accountability.

> *If we don't change the direction*
> *we are headed, we will end*
> *up where we are going.*
> *—Jodi Picoult*

A good PLAN anticipates and clarifies each of the next steps of Do, Check, and Adjust. When a written PLAN and the D, C, and A steps that follow are completed, it is a great motivator to celebrate success, take on the next challenge, and use **PDCA** at an even higher level of capacity.

> *Pursuing opportunities or problem*
> *solving without PDCA is like*
> *mud wrestling with a pig.*
> *You get tired, the pig gets tired. You*
> *get muddy, the pig gets muddy.*
> *Time passes. The pig wins,*
> *and the pig likes it.*

D = DO

Oh, this is easy. We all know how to DO things. The challenge is to actually DO what we said in our written PLAN—nothing more and nothing less. If we deviate from our PLAN, then we won't really know if the PLAN was any good or not. Then the written PLAN was not the real PLAN, was it?

There can be many very good reasons to deviate from the PLAN; for example, when you find the PLAN was flawed, perhaps not specific enough, short of resources, or some critical element was left out. At that point, put down your DO tools and go back and refine your PLAN. This is the essence of adaptive management. **PDCA** is the key to success.

Changing our PLAN is a good outcome because we learned from it, and now we are smarter than when we started. Ahhhh Learning, the first big step on our quest. We had to be accountable in order to admit that the PLAN was flawed. This should be celebrated as a success! Accumulated wisdom from a steady diet of sometimes painful learning is the goal. This is system capacity building: the capacity of understanding the system we are working with.

Now you have completed the first trip around the **PDCA** cycle, since in the process of actually testing your PLAN, you learned something that drove you to adapt the PLAN to reality, thus making it and you more effective! This is simultaneously learning, being accountable, and improving on the path to higher performance.

You'll never get bored when
you try something new.
There's really no limit to
what you can do.
—Dr. Seuss

And of course, you had to be accountable in order to acknowledge the PLAN was flawed. This can be a hard habit to master, but a critical one. Then resume DO on the newly documented PLAN. Try it again. Keep re-cycling till your PLAN meets the challenge, solves the problem, etc.

Accountability is likely the largest area of concern for leaders. This is where the rubber meets the road. All the planning in the world can't overcome a lack of discipline following the plan to its completion. This is the Achilles' heel in most organizations. If you are not accountable yourself to yourself and others, then don't expect that from others. Don't bother making plans you do not or cannot complete. If during an early test of your plan you find you won't be able to complete it as written, stop and get it right before expending any more resources on a PLAN that will not take you all the way to your planned goal.

If you run into barriers, re-cycle back through each of the four **PDCA** steps. YES, all the way to writing down/editing the changed PLAN. The more you cycle through the steps, the more proficient, efficient, speedy, and effective you will become at this PLAN and actually with all future PLANS. This is the essence of adaptive management. I am looking for more CASA discipline (Consistent And Systematic Application) in our actions than most people are applying these days. It takes discipline and practice. Like learning to ride a bike or roller-skate, each attempt brings us closer to mastery.

Document the revised PLAN before you return to DO. That first revision was the first learning and PLAN improvement, the first trip around the PDCA cycle. That was the first of many successes! Now you are already at a higher level of understanding and thus capacity than when you started. That effort alone shows the learning circle and process improvement is in play. The second/revised and improved PLAN will be better by the learning we got from our first failed attempt at DO. This is not a failure. Each time you rewrite a PLAN, you become more effective.

What if you failed the critical leadership behavior accountability test? What if, when faced with the first clue the PLAN was flawed, you decided to still proceed with no changes to the PLAN? What would you have shown others by this move? You might as well give up now as you have shown by this very lack of discipline that you are not really up to the logic of steady PLAN refinement and adaptive management.

If, just by luck, we actually succeed on our first attempt, we may decide wrongly that we are better and smarter than we actually are. We are looking to build a stream of successes every time we build and perform a PLAN. We want a reputation as a person who sets a PLAN and completes it. A good outcome would be that we and others begin to see that we are getting better and better and better at building and performing our PLANS over time, demonstrating the continuous process improvement logic. The learning is new for each attempt. Think of the discipline this will take. Think of the new level of accountability you and your organization can then count on going forward. If you can master this for yourself, you have moved a long way to later helping others master it.

> *The difference between what*
> *we get and what we expected*
> *is the margin of learning.*
> —*Rich Marovich, Putah Creek*
> *Streamkeeper, Emeritus*

Some call this failing forward or failing upward. I like the idea that if it were followed with CASA, it would be the essence of true adaptive management. Subsequent trials will lead to yet more learnings, each time bringing us closer and closer to our goal of an effective PLAN. Remember, we are trying to (1) learn how to solve problems or master challenges more effectively, (2) be accountable for our hand in the work, and (3) deliver ever increasingly valuable performance outcomes.

For most of us, DO is the easiest step by far. We tend to get a lot of psychological reinforcement from DO. We get a sense of action, a sense of accomplishment, a chance to practice and exhibit our skills, something we can show to others—at least we are DOing something! In fact, most of us are "stuck on DO" at the expense of the other needed steps in the **PDCA** model for success. We will talk more about this later as we move along to building the eight-step template.

As expected, DO does take up most of our time anyway. It is the action part of all work. No problem, unless we are so "stuck on DO" that we fail to adequately take the other critical steps in the learning cycle. Broken **PDCA** cycles lead to never-ending Band-Aids, work-arounds pasted on work-arounds!

Once DO is over, we risk a broken **PDCA** cycle if we then just move on to the next problem or opportunity. Some people get stuck in the PLAN-DO, PLAN-DO, PLAN-DO loop and never get to the learnings available in the CHECK-ADJUST phases. This is called the doom loop as we are doomed to just repeat any failures again and again. CHECKing and ADJUSTing may have been able to save us from having to repeat this over again in the future.

Now that we did what we said we would do in our written PLAN, nothing more and nothing less, let's CHECK it against the PLAN. Think of Einstein's definition of insanity.

C = CHECK

Once we DO what the PLAN called for exactly, nothing more and nothing less, then let's CHECK to see how well the PLAN actually worked. This takes more accountability discipline. Did we achieve the stated objective? Did we actually follow the PLAN? Did we use the resources we had planned, not more or less resources? Were there unanticipated resource needs or unexpected consequences?

What did we learn about our planning skills and ourselves in the process? This last question is critical because we want to (1) learn to PLAN, (2) DO what we planned, (3) CHECK with honest accountability, (4) ADJUST for the next time. We want to provide valuable performance outcomes. We want to get better and better and better at building capacity in our systems so that we don't later need even more problem-solving.

There is a tendency for all of us to be knowers rather than learners. Our egos love to be fanned with stories of the wisdom we have accumulated from our life's experiences. If we are too fixated on what we know, we will fail to hold the learner's mindset of curiosity. Think of a toddler learning to climb the stairs; they have a learner's mindset.

As soon as the initial DO phase is over, we all usually want to move quickly on to the next new challenge as we always have so much pressing work. Unfortunately, we don't go back and document what actually happened or what it took to make it happen.

If we fail to consider carefully and record what we learned and where our accountability plan was weak, we won't have this information next time we are faced with this or a similar challenge. All those involved may have much different ideas of what the learnings are. What if everyone impacted or involved came away with completely different ideas of what happened, what was learned, and how to improve plans in the future? I tend to think this outcome is all too common. This is a leadership behavioral challenge. You are tasked with getting the work done, why not also build the capacity to do work?

The CHECK phase is the cure of this failing. CHECKing with discipline what we did, how it worked, who did or did not do what by when is the way to see if this was the best way to meet the challenge. It will tell us what we learned for use next time. This is a critical personal and group behavior for growth in understanding leading to learning, accountability, and improved performance.

Many high-performance organizations have learned to perform "Postmortems" or "After-Action Reviews" for the

CHECK part of the learning cycle. These are excellent, and many useful models are easily accessible. These are also useful for individuals. Look this up on the internet. In addition, some high-performance leaders and organizations have begun to conduct "Premortems" as part of the PLAN phase as a planning challenge to better anticipate what risks or potential unanticipated and unintended consequences might arise. I urge you to learn more about this as well.

These tools are powerful for individuals and leaders and indispensable for groups. We are usually in such a hurry to get moving due to the nature of some looming failure or some huge missed opportunity that we start working before we even know exactly what the root challenge really is. This is a leadership failure that wastes resources and time as the potential for misdirection of focus is high. This is a place to practice the five Whys.

For a lifetime, I have heard the old saying, "There is never enough time to do it right, but always enough time to do it over." The cost of rework is huge. What if you and your organization could reduce rework by, say, just 5 percent? And what if you did it by being more effective at everything you attempt due to increased discipline using **PDCA**?

> *Good judgment comes from*
> *experience and experience*
> *comes from bad judgment.*
> *—Rita Mae Broom*

Sure, you would seemingly spend more time up front making good PLANs, but you would get that investment back and much more in reduced rework and reduction in lost time. If, in the new more disciplined process, you also learned how to avoid some planning flaws, your next approach would be much smarter. This can become a virtuous cycle, leading to more success for more people more often.

What if by your example others became more effective in their work and then your collective work? What if the culture around disciplined learning was so reinforcing, everyone wanted to be part of the effort to make and implement great PLANs? What if reviews of our work were less tied to publicity for individual heroes or fools and more tied to our collective capacity to build and perform great PLANs together?

> *Pay me now, or pay me even more later!*
> *—Unknown*

The CHECK phase should end with a list of clear and useful learnings to apply going forward. Why do all this work and not capture how it could have been done faster, at lower cost, on time, conserving more resources, with higher quality, happier workers, and happy customers and stakeholders?

When quality CHECKing becomes a habit, personal and organizational capacities are enhanced toward higher performance. Once embedded in the culture, you will find individuals becoming more disciplined about their CHECKing skills and specific work and groups to be much more willing to go on the learning journeys of discovery together. People look to their leaders for guidance, useful examples of smart thinking, and inspiration. What if your approach to work showed them the way?

Our egos can take a big painful hit during the CHECK step if we see flaws that point to individuals. If we can tell ourselves and each other the truth without blame, we can focus on the process and not the players. On the other hand, we can also get a big ego boost, especially if we find we actually did follow the PLAN and got the intended outcome. This requires a deep level of authenticity and vulnerability; both lead to higher-quality leadership.

Fix the system, not blame those
who played by the rules and lost.

While this chapter is about individual learning, now is a good time to share that smart leaders know to make the CHECK step a safe zone where we work to fix the problem and not the blame. Failings or missed opportunities need to be viewed by everyone as learning opportunities that lead to future success. After all, most of us might have made the same misstep.

Not the devil made me do it!
The system made me do it!

A = ADJUST

Now that the CHECK phase is complete, it is time to see how the learnings can be useful to raise the bar of performance in the next attempt, the next PLAN, the next challenge. The results of the CHECK cycle need to be expressed specifically in terms of how the PLAN or some key process steps will be improved the next time we approach a similar challenge.

> *Frequently, learnings from a*
> *CHECK phase on one project will*
> *be of good use on other projects*
> *since the systems failings are usually*
> *patterns of failed human behavior.*

What did we accomplish, and what did we learn that we can use going forward? What did not go according to PLAN? What can we do better next time with an improved PLAN? Think of the **PDCA** cycle as an ascending spiral ramp. If we did it right, we should be able to see the new elements in the next PLAN that emerged from the CHECK and ADUST phases from this attempt as we ascend the spiral ramp. This is called continuous process improvement or Adaptive Management.

This kind of positive progression in capacity only happens if we are both aware of the content of our work and the process of our work. What is the system behind the work? See figure 3.

Figure 3

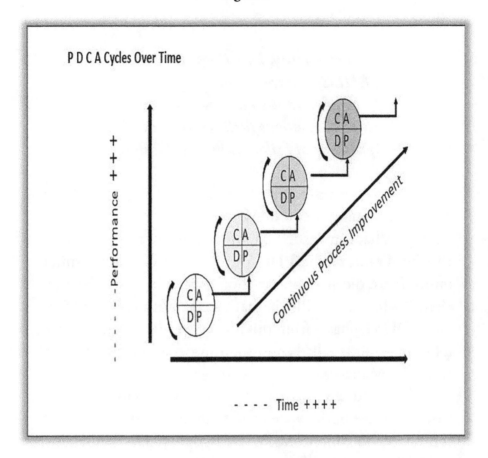

Each time we take a step to the next **PDCA** iteration, we are ascending the spiral ramp of improvements and better performance, closer and closer toward our goal. Each time we are taking what we learned and reinvesting that in our next attempt both in content and equally important in process. Each time we are learning our way to higher levels of performance, and we are learning how to be better learners. See figure 4.

Figure 4

Take time to study how the ramp climbs clockwise around the cycle. First PLAN, then DO, then CHECK, then ADJUST, then on to the next PLAN at a higher level of performance. The rise is the improvement in understanding and thus capacity over time. This is the essence of applied learning now called adaptive management. Next, see figure 5.

Figure 5

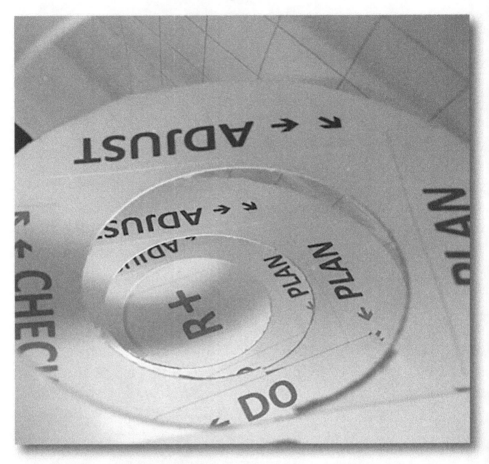

Each succeeding trip around the ascending cycle will bring stronger, smarter, more efficient effort. The R+ in the center of the bottom is to signify the positive reinforcement feedback (R+) needed to sustain continued **PDCA** cycles toward better and better outcomes. In order to smoothly ascend the learning spiral, participants need lots of positive reinforcement for taking the sometimes painful steps of being vulnerable and exposing the places where they were less than perfect. Again, here is where positive reinforcement matters. You can read more about this in *Bringing Out the Best in People* by Aubrey C. Daniels, PhD.

The key here for leaders is to show by example that studying our PLANS and DOings to reveal the opportunities for improvements is the path to learning, accountability, and high performance.

R+ is needed because this is hard work. Oh, it is not hard, really; it just takes a lot of personal humility and discipline to move out of our old sloppy habits toward habits of more accountable high performance. Each step requires focus, discipline, and energy. Each step leads us around and up the ascending learning cycle up toward higher and higher levels of performance.

Actually, the work we DO will not likely be any more effort or difficult than we would have done anyway. The big difference is we are DOing better-defined work to test the PLAN in our quest to (1) learn, (2) be accountable, and (3) get good outcomes. So we are no longer just doing our work; we are building our capacity to do our work as well.

P D C B?

But wait, there is more! I will never forget when I heard of P D C B for the first time. We can have **PDCA**, or we can have PDCB! See figure 6.

Figure 6

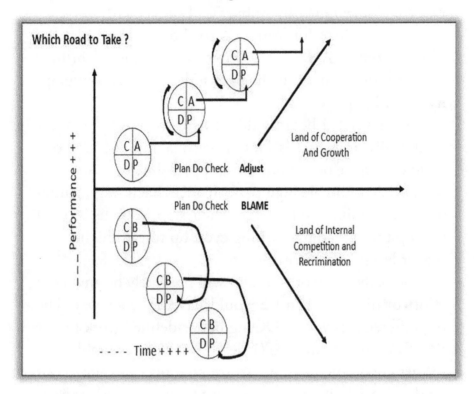

By their behaviors the leader sets the stage for the choice between the land of cooperation, growth, and high discretionary effort (**PDCA**) or the land of internal competition and recrimination (PDCB).

Once a group learns which way project reviews are handled, the die is cast. From then on, each trip around the cycle can either be hiding errors and delays and preparing for the worst, or sharing errors and delays and learning ways to ensure they do not happen again.

Which will it be for you and your organization? **PDCA** or PDCB?

The **PDCA** cycle seems simple and easy to use. But it is initially hard to use because it calls for more personal and deep disciplined behavior than most of us are used to practicing. It calls for new behaviors, which people find hard to sustain. Initially, it takes more time and seems clunky. But once you make it a habit, it becomes much simpler and easy to use. It becomes the norm: the way we think, the way we align our efforts, the way we work.

If you want to know who is responsible, look in your mirror!

PDCA can simplify how to approach most all challenges. The secret is to have cultural behavioral processes where this wisdom of a systematic approach to learning and capacity building is embedded in the steps we routinely take, embedded in the PLAN. We will cover this in more depth in later chapters.

One common question is how to do we teach and embed this in our organization? The answer is simple: when a new person enters an organization, they very quickly adapt to the "way things are done around here." So you never need to teach this specifically to each new person arriving if everyone here is already doing it. New people will very quickly adapt to the organization's existing processes whatever they are, disciplined or sloppy.

The hard part is how to get those already here to learn and practice the new ways with consistent and systematic application (CASA). That is where true authentic leadership comes in.

In my experience and study, there are two major ways of embedding such new behaviors in an organization. You can lead, teach, preach, and slowly drag or coax people to new behaviors till they come to believe the new behaviors may be better, or you can make abrupt imposed changes to drive new behaviors, requiring use of the new systems, and then work with people as they gradually adapt to new beliefs.

So you can work to change beliefs with the expectation new behaviors will become the norm, or enforce changed behaviors then hope beliefs in the new way will follow. I have been victim and perpetrator of both attempts many times. I think the first approach, at the outset, seems more humane and socially acceptable on the surface, except I think it rarely ever works. People just resist change either intentionally or unintentionally. This kind of change can take forever. Perhaps you don't have forever. It takes a very persistent and patient leader to ever make this work.

> *I didn't think this up, so I will sit*
> *back and see if it will ever work.*
> *vs.*
> *I have been told I must make this*
> *work, might as well get started.*

The second approach sets up immediate new performance expectations, teaches the new ways, and sets forth and provides kind yet firm consequences for lack of performance. This way seems much harsher, and many leaders don't have the guts or persistence to take such seemingly drastic steps, except I think it is about the only effective way to make important changes in behavior. Organizational culture change is a huge subject. I urge you to study up on the various ways to proceed. I have spent several decades studying this. I am convinced the second way is the only effective path if it is done correctly.

So the two approaches are lead, teach, prod, and hope, or force and support with consequences both positive or negative. I have come to appreciate the old saying "Fake it till you make it." I think this means set up and require the new behaviors, despite the pushback, and practice them with discipline till everyone comes to believe they are the best ones. Some may never get aligned. Perhaps they should be working somewhere else?

> *Seeing is believing, so let's see it in action so we can believe it will work.*
> *—Unknown*

You are the leader. You will have to decide which road to take. In the first method, you are granting time and patience till people come around to some new thinking and conclusions if they ever do. In the second method, once the new behavioral expectations are in place, you will need to grant some time and patience while people catch up to what is now expected of them.

Be kind but firm. Some will want to seek your sympathy; that's fine, yet you need to mind the higher long-term objectives. Be the leader who can lead the people to higher levels of learning, accountability, and performance by your example. Some people never want to grow up and deal with reality. They are usually not chosen to lead. I believe the second method is faster and more effective and more humane in the long run.

> ***When the going gets tough,***
> ***the tough get going.***
> ***—Joseph Kennedy***

It's okay to be the boss! If you were promoted to a position of leadership, then act like it! You didn't promote yourself, did you? You were selected based on some criteria (best choice, least bad, only choice, I don't know). Now you have the role of moving the work of the organization forward.

> ***Managers work in the system.***
> ***Leaders work on the system.***
> ***—Unknown***

This role calls for making realistic assessments of the capacity of your systems to actually do what is necessary. There is the physical system like machines, warehouses, factories, etc., and there is the human side of the system, the people. Usually, the biggest leverage is in the human side of the system.

Machines, warehouses, and factories don't do anything till the humans show up. It is easy and frequently too common to complain about the physical parts of our system since that is less threatening. Yet it is the human side of our systems, which is much harder to deal with, where most all the leverage for learning, accountability, and performance exists.

It's okay to be the boss! Organizations need leadership. If you are the boss, then be a good boss. Bosses have the role of being the judge of performance. If you are a judge, then be a good judge. How do you want to be judged? Do you want to be led by someone who fails to deal with conflict?

Do you want to be led by someone who lets things fester into internal competition, descending into chaos? Do you want to be led by someone who just wants to take the easy road and make everyone happy while ignoring the larger challenges faced by the organization? You can do that easily by just telling each person what they want to hear instead of what is needed from them. That way they can fight it out down the hall in never-ending skirmishes instead of getting a firm crisp and final answer from the boss. What would be your best overall contribution to the effectiveness of the organization over time?

**The competition is out
there, not in here.**

Laying out clear plans for the work is critical. That is your role as leader. Next time you take an airplane flight, think of the pilot in the cockpit and their checklist process, the process instruction manual. Your life depends on this being complete, correct, and followed every time. You expect nothing less. What about space flight? Do you think they are diligent about specific plans followed closely? The airline industry has brought the **PDCA** process of detailed checklist PLANS to an amazing level of safety.

It's a sure cinch your pilot did not have a hand in writing this specific checklist they are working from today that your life depends on. It was developed over many decades with many steady improvements likely caused by past near misses or failures. They do not have to know about all that or even believe that each step is important. On the other hand, they do have to follow it to the letter. This is enforced behavior that may eventually come to deep shared belief. I think pilots would all agree the checklists and their strict use save lives.

The medical world operates on the same principles. Let's hope your next medical procedure is conducted with rigor that does not allow the surgeon to cut off the wrong part! Think of the last time you had surgery, and different people along the process kept asking you some of the same questions over and over. They want to be sure they get it right, and so do you. The enhanced performance of modern medicine, vehicles, phones, TVs, computers, etc., are examples of continuous process improvement based on the application of **PDCA**. These processes take discipline.

> *Such processes are in use wherever*
> *lives are at stake. Why not adapt*
> *them to your life and operations?*

Many fields of human endeavor have taken these steps to new heights of performance. Can you learn to practice similar step-by-step discipline in your own work? You know this is true, but most of us find it very hard to move to the more disciplined approach even though it will differentiate us from our competition, both personally and organizationally. CASA is the key.

PLANning and DOing are concrete activities that many like since they create a sense of forward progress, and they allow us to show others our hard work. It is easy to get hooked on the adrenaline of PLANning and DOing. PLANning and DOing are clearly action-oriented activities. These can provide a real-time sense of progress.

Unfortunately, CHECKing and ADJUSTing are abstract activities. They seem to take time away from the perceived real work and require deeper reflection, honesty, and truth. Many feel uncomfortable working in this abstract area of the cycle since there is a feeling we are wasting time we could be using to actually be DOing something. It's as if assessing our process is not worthy of our time.

Finally ADJUSTing is a more surface thought process. One has to take what was learned in P, D, and C and figure out how to best use it in the next PLAN. Not everyone is good at synthesizing what was learned into the next PLAN.

Some people are good at PLANning. Some are best at DOing. Some are good at CHECKing. And some are good at ADJUSTing. Few are good at all these. If you buy into the need for all four key steps, you will want to plan your own work to include all four steps. You will move toward more disciplined work process for your own work.

As an aside, smart leaders tend to look for this same diversity of thinking in the people they hire. What if your people were collectively naturally good at all four focus areas? What if you made hire decisions partly on this factor? Should you hire to fill gaps in your organization's **PDCA** capacity?

Perhaps you can do some deep reflection now and come to terms with which of the four steps are the most comfortable for you? Perhaps you now can recognize you may have been unaware or ignoring steps that can now be seen as obstacles to your own success? Who do you need working with you to counteract your own favorite yet limited approaches?

Before we move on, I want to diverge a bit with some general thoughts about learning and changing behaviors. Learning new things can seem so hard. When faced with new learning, we struggle to understand that there's nothing basically wrong with us. Learning new things can be hard and be the path to ever more satisfying lives.

> *No guts, no glory.*
> *—Frederick Corbin Blesse*

Think back to learning to roller-skate, ride a bike, or play the ukulele. We do it wrong till we do it right. We can learn at any time, but only if we are ready to take the risk. It always feels weird and impossible at first, but we keep trying, failing, trying, getting hurt, trying again. Finally, it seems easy.

Why do toddlers approach learning with wonder, and adults approach learning with fear? Our egos are at stake. Take the stance of a "learner" as opposed to the stance of a "knower," and the learning will be much easier. This is how behavior change happens, and we suffer when we forget this.

We mistakenly think of behavior change as always more effective if self-initiated from the inside. But at the root level, behavior change most easily and effectively starts from the outside. If it starts from inside, it is because we came to some new thinking about the need for change by ourselves. That is change driven from the inside, albeit coping with pressures or new realizations from the outside. Perhaps the only difference is one of timing?

Rapid change usually happens from the outside in. This is good because we know how to learn about and make behavioral changes on the outside before we come to the belief that the new way is best. We have been doing this all our lives. There is an old saying, "Fake it till you make it." Do the new thing despite its unfamiliarity till it becomes our way. We don't usually easily embrace the much deeper thinking/belief set that would drive new behaviors.

> *The greatest waste of our natural resources is the number of people who never achieve their potential. Get out of the slow lane; shift into the fast one. If you think you can't, you won't. If you think you can, you just might. Even making the effort will make you seem like a new person. Reputations are made by searching for things that can't be done and doing them. Aim low: boring. Aim high: soaring!*
> *—Unattributed quote shared from good friend Doug Aldrich*

First, think about where you want to end up. Let's say you were able to change a lot. Where would that take you?

What would you now be able to do then that you cannot yet do? How would you know you'd changed? What would you notice? What behaviors would other people notice? This is the power of an inspiring and compelling vision.

Second, persistently do the new behaviors, even though you are out of your element, that will bring about the change you seek, even if the new behaviors feel unnatural. Persistently take steady small but real steps toward the right direction every day, even if they are not perfect and feel foreign or challenging. It is more important to do something now than to plan for future greatness and never take a step.

Third, ignore the fact that in spite of your efforts, you don't feel changed yet. Ignore the voices of failure in your head. Fake it till you make it.

Fourth, keep practicing and refining the new behaviors you want to be known for till they actually become the new you. Many have done this, and so can you. All it takes is desire and discipline.

Think BE – DO – HAVE.

Let's say you want a million-dollar lifestyle = HAVE

In order to HAVE this, you have to actually DO something that others will pay a million dollars for = DO

In order to DO this, you have to BE a person who can and does this = BE

BE – DO – HAVE

For our consideration here, if you want to HAVE an organizational culture of learning, accountability, and performance, you have to DO the behaviors that bring this about, and you have to BE the person who can and routinely does those things.

In the end, behaviors and success come from who you are (= BE), not from your intentions of better actions (= DO) or intentions of better things (= HAVE). This applies to those who want to be pro ball players, TV personalities, great fishermen, inspiring leaders, etc.

Finally, one day you will wake up and realize that you have been changed by all this effort. They say it takes sixty-six times practicing a new behavior before it is close to becoming a habit; "The way we do things," so think long game.

> ***Learning is being changed***
> ***by the experience.***
> ***—Unknown***

A longtime very successful executive and very close friend, in reviewing drafts for this book, asked an important question: "What role does intuition or gut play in the learning process as this is what a lot of folks rely on as their primary decision-making criteria?"

A great question.

The "knower" in us relies on intuition and gut feel. The newly emerging "Learner" in us knows better. The gut thinking that got us here did not get us to where we now need to be; it only got us here. That thinking came out of our intuition and gut. What new thinking do we need now to move toward the results we now seek? Maybe some new facts would help?

I think we can't ever put down our intuition or gut in thinking about the challenges we face, no matter how hard we try. Humans are sense makers. Our brains are wired to draw conclusions from our experience. Those accumulated conclusions are then front and center in our thinking about new information. In fact, I think this may be one of our biggest challenges as leaders—to let the facts lead us to conclusions and not make conclusions and then go looking for data to support what our gut tells us. We have all experienced this in others. Let's not make this our way of being.

This behavioral error is called confirmation bias. Go look that up as you need to know about it to avoid it. A confirmation bias is a type of cognitive bias that involves favoring information that confirms previously existing beliefs or biases. For example, imagine that a person holds a belief that left-handed people are more creative than right-handed people. Perhaps they themselves are left-handed. Worse, what if then they act on this conclusion at the exclusion of far more than half the population?

I urge you to look up confirmation bias as part of your learning journey to fully understand how misguided it can be. I have been sharing my thoughts on the need for discipline in applying the wisdom of the scientific method. **PDCA** means putting down our intuition and ignoring our guts to let the facts drive our thinking and actions.

Chapter Summary

This chapter described the fundamental learning cycle in detail for an individual and how it is used to improve ourselves and our processes over time. With this foundation, we can now move on to how groups learn on our way to understanding the eight-step template, which is described in chapter 5.

CHAPTER 3

――― ❦ ―――

PDCA: A Mental Model for How Groups Learn

Chapter Summary

This chapter expands on the basic four-step **PDCA** foundation for individuals to the fundamental learning cycle for groups and how it is used to improve organizations and processes over time. The basic process should now be familiar and may seem repetitive, but know that it is important to see how it is much more complex and powerful than for just one brain.

An important part of group learning is how the individuals in the group think. Before we start talking about group learning, let's talk more about brain styles. If we are working alone, then we only need to consult our own brain—so easy and yet so limited! However, most work is done in concert with others as suppliers, customers, coworkers, and collaborators.

Being able to collaborate is a critical ability in order for an individual, team, group, and organization to succeed. How do we collectively practice learning, being accountable, and performing when so much depends on our collaboration with others?

Teamwork is a whole bunch of
people doing what I say!
(See how far that will get
you in the long run.)

Certainly, we have all learned, sometimes by humbling painful experiences, that we think in certain ways and clearly others think differently. Sometimes it is impossible to figure out what others are thinking or what drove their conclusions, so different from our own with apparently the same inputs. It is so easy to just discount those who think differently as uninformed, ill-intentioned, incapable of seeing what we see, or worse. But what if they are actually seeing things correctly, and we are missing something, something critical?

An understanding of brain styles is a great way to open our minds to better understanding and working with others. We each have unique ways of interpreting the world, approaching challenges, holding our mental models, and valuing others. A common way to discuss this is to say someone is left-brain or right-brain dominant. This has gotten some press and traction in the past few years. This is just one of many models of brain style. According to the model, left-brain dominance is associated with people who tend to be more logical, analytical, linear, more narrowly focused fact seekers. I don't think for a moment it is this simple, but models can be helpful even if knowingly limited.

Right-brain dominance is associated more with people who are more holistic in their thinking, taking into account a wider range of facts but also the whole complexity of an issue, including emotions. Left brain is more the realm of those who are more directly focused on the issue at hand, more directly analytical. The reality that all this is in play while we work alone or with others is amazing. I call this the human side of the system, and it is routinely ignored by many. No one style is best, and all are important.

No one brain is totally one-sided, but we each have preferred ways of thinking and being. This is not a book about brain styles. I am not an expert in this field. There are a variety of other equally useful models of brain styles and ways of thinking. I encourage you to read up on this field as it can make a huge difference in your openness to others and ability to collaborate, leading to your long-term success and life happiness. I recommend you read *The Creative Brain* by Ned Herrmann as a start.

Another model I like and have used for years is the "Meyers Briggs" test and framework as outlined in the book *Please Understand Me* by David Keirsey and Marilyn Bates. I like it as it does a good job of surfacing the differences between introverts and extroverts and the impact on communications and culture. No one model is best in my view, but having a clear dominant mental model that others can and do regularly think much differently than we do is very, very important. After all, they may be right.

Some people are pretty centered, capable of being analytical and holistic at the same time. Some people live at the far extremes of the ranges, serious and analytical to a fault, or more interested in feelings and holistic to a fault. This is much too simple a summary, but you get the idea. We will encounter all these types in our lives and work.

Some people are relatively flexible. Some are very ridged. Some are quick to learn, and some are slow to learn. Some just want to go along, no matter where it leads. Stress tends to heighten these differences. All these things matter in how groups function. What is the collective wisdom possible from the brains on your team?

> *No one of us is as smart as all of us.*
> *—Kenneth H. Blanchard*

It seems to me the more extreme the brain style, the less flexible a person tends to be. To effectively collaborate, we need to have a way of interacting and honoring the input of all styles. We are all capable of moving out of our comfort zone with others, but only if we feel respected, trusted, and safe ourselves.

A learning culture where both facts and feelings are considered can promote the trust and openness we all need to be operating at our collective best. The issue is how do we actually think and act when the chips are down, and we are under stress and out of our comfort zone? I call this our "first out" response as that is how we normally act and how others will perceive us when we first encounter some new idea or challenge. This is what we will normally bring to any group interactions.

> *We are what we repeatedly do*
> *(even though we may be*
> *capable of better!).*

Even if we work in a team with others who share our own preferred brain style, we need to interact, cooperate, collaborate, and serve groups or individuals that will likely have different brain-style profiles. More importantly, we frequently have sponsors, suppliers, peers, subordinates, or customers who think differently than our personal brain style prefers. Our success may depend on the sponsorship or support of our "Customers." Whatever we come up with has to pass the test of acceptance by others with perhaps much different ways of thinking about the issue.

> *No customer no business, no business no job,*
> *no job no money, no money no eats.*
> *—Herb Wimmer Sr.*

We need to be aware and understand our own way of thinking and being in the world and improve our sensitivity to the brain styles of others, leading to more effective interaction skills. There is a natural tendency to think our brain style is best. Forget that. No one brain style is best for all challenges.

The smart people learn early we need to make room for all the styles to truly be successful as individuals and certainly in teams, groups, and organizations. While I have used the left-brain–right-brain model here, there are a number of other valuable ways to think about human ranges of thinking and being.

I urge you to learn more about this field to open your mind to acceptance of others who think and act differently than you do. As alternatives to left-brain–right-brain model, look for more information in *The Leadership Equation* by Lee and Norma Barr, PhD. Being aware of brain styles will improve your personal and group sensitivity and performance.

With this as important background, let's move on to **PDCA** in groups.

We know individuals can learn. We can learn and then practice behaviors that increase the rate at which we personally learn and improve our performance. A much more important question is whether groups, teams, and organizations can increase their collective rate of learning. Much has been written about this. I recommend *Learning Organizations* by Fred Kofman et al. Can your organization continually improve the rate at which it is learning and improving?

Can teams, units, departments, and whole organizations ascend to ever higher levels of embedded and practiced accountability and performance over time? I think that is the path to much higher organizational performance. What if the culture of your organization had continuous learning and capacity building at its core? I recommend you review *The Fifth Discipline Fieldbook* by Peter Senge et al. for additional deeper insights and some useful tools.

We are all getting older every day. Are we getting wiser every day? What is the rate of learning for us? Are we getting older faster than we are getting wiser or vice versa? Do you know more now, and are you more capable than you were, say, five or ten years ago? What could you do to improve the rate or your own and group learning so you arrived at useful wisdom sooner? It will likely take being more open to ideas we have not yet been able to understand or embrace.

What about the groups we work in? Are we as a group becoming collectively more capable over time, a "Learning Organization"? What about our competition? Are they on a steeper and thus more effective learning curve in their collective work? Even if we are an agency or organization that does not really have any direct competitors, are we learning fast enough to keep up with all the new emerging challenges?

Learning is not guaranteed. Learning requires openness and vulnerability. Continuous learning in groups requires an open learning culture and embedded learning processes like **PDCA**. Unfortunately, it is possible for a group to become collectively less wise by the addition or departure of members who do not share this understanding.

> *Unless you are learning faster*
> *than your competition,*
> *the end is in sight.*
> *—Unknown*

Increasing the rate of organizational learning is easy to say, but very hard to actually do. Actually, I think learning is going on all the time. The question is, is it fast enough and effective enough? Does it bring you success, or do you struggle just to keep up…or worse? I do think it is possible to continually move toward becoming a learning organization with higher levels of group effectiveness if the leaders can make the critical behaviors a leadership habit. An open trusting culture, leadership behaviors that promote learning from fact-based trials, and the **PDCA** cycle are the key.

> *There is rarely ever a scarcity of money or plans, only a scarcity of high enough confidence in those plans. The key to building confidence is to build a reputation that you do whatever you say you are going to do and not promise to do what you cannot do.*
> *—Unknown*

Perhaps you have had the gift of working in a place and for someone who valued learning as the path to higher output. Perhaps you had a chance to experience this feeling and then had to move on. Once you experience the power of this culture, you will be in search of finding it or creating it again wherever you go.

Remember, the information you need to get the learning is always there standing right behind the output, but it can only be useful if it is identified and then used to make output even better. The learning is free and valuable to those who are smart enough to recognize and capture it.

The big challenge is the behaviors that drive a culture dedicated to learning. Can the people in the system regularly and truthfully and more fully share their opinions and observations, or are those important expressions being limited by the culture? Are mistakes and process failures seen as learning opportunities, or do heads have to roll? Do leaders routinely seek and value information new to them and change to opinions that may differ from where they started? Are they able to work with group members who ask the tough questions?

> **Should we pay less attention to those who disagree with us, or pay more attention to those who agree? Where is the most learning likely to come from?**

Are group members able to respect and work effectively with leaders who hold differing opinions in a collaborative learning way? Is it dangerous to tell your truth? Are people driven to act as if they know things when they don't because to not know is to not be successful or worse? Give yourself a treat and look up the "Dunning Kruger Effect" on the internet. You may find it interesting. While you are at it, look up "Imposter Syndrome." See if you can select a satisfactory place for yourself between these two. Do that now.

> **The most important thing in communications is to hear what isn't being said.**
> **—Peter Drucker**

The big fear is falling into groupthink. If you are not familiar with that term, go look it up now. Some team members can fall into the habit of lazy thinking, just going along so they don't have to tax their own mental reserves to ensure success. We can't just rely on the wisdom of the crowd. Sometimes they are wrong. Pointed questions that drive the team to justify the final position are critical to success. A good practice is to challenge some members to play "devil's advocate" to find the flaws in the plan now before it is too late.

> *One of the interesting things*
> *about poor judgment is*
> *we do not know we have*
> *it till it is too late.*
> *—Unknown*

These are measures of the "sharing space" between us. This is the human side of the system. The learning occurs because the sharing space is safe, welcoming, and futures seeking. Can we turn away from criticism of what is in favor of focusing on what could be if we collectively set on a path to learn together by trying the next new thing?

> *Where would we be*
> *without our dreams?*
> *—Gerald Howell, Famous*
> *Barbecue Philosopher*

You might want to take time to explore "Six Thinking Hats." The six thinking hats is a method used to amplify creative conversations by making sure that a broad variety of viewpoints and thinking styles are represented. Using six roles (or "hats"), the framework—developed by Dr.

Edward de Bono—allows teams to more easily structure abstract thinking for productive results.

Learning cultures are primarily driven by the behaviors of leaders in thousands of little ways. Can leaders inspire others to dare to dream? Can leaders make it safe to challenge the current prevailing way of operating? Do leaders have the patience, wisdom, humility, and capacity to live in the messy world of the unknown, inspire a learning culture, and not take every question as a challenge to their authority?

> *Inspiring leaders don't find the path, they engage with others to cocreate the path to success.*
> *—Unknown*

A **PDCA** model for more than one person follows the same path as for a single brain, but each step is much more complicated by the needed interaction of more brains and brain styles. The participants need to be able to express their truths without repercussion. The steps require true unfettered sharing and collaboration. Figure 7 shows the cycle for individuals embedded inside the cycle for groups. Next, we will explore the **PDCA** learning cycle for a group.

Figure 7

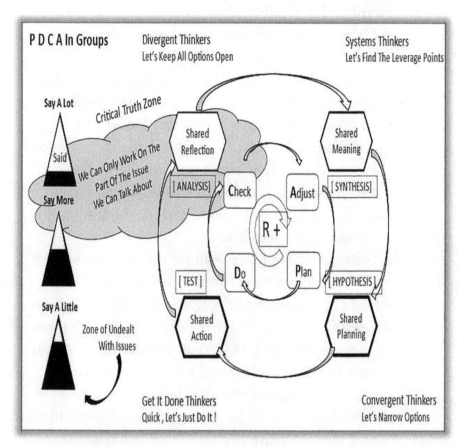

There may be a tendency to think collaboration in planning needs to always be smooth and congenial. On the contrary, the best ideas are hard fought and vetted by those who care, really care, about the outcomes. This calls for understanding that good outcomes will prevail through the civil yet stressful path of disagreements. What if you were in a meeting where everyone simply agreed to what was being proposed? Would you be worried? I would. I have later found how little alignment there actually was when the PLAN failed.

We need to be expressing our own thoughts about the path forward and be flexible, open to new realities, our own personal learning, and seeking a good acceptable solution rather than a perfect solution.

Don't expect historic rivalries to be discarded or tensions resolved. Fundamental differences in worldview, personality, and brain style will remain. Understand that despite these natural tensions, a path forward can be forged using **PDCA** and the eight-step template. Show the path by being the person who can behave in ways that facilitate co-creation. We need to co-create a path to the future, not battle out whose path to follow.

The behavior of the leader will set the tone for what is possible. Adam Kahane has written some very useful books on collaboration. The role of the leader is usually to find a way to get people to work together. What if you were more informed about the ways that true collaboration could become more frequent and embedded in your culture?

What if people agreed and collaborated on this issue, even though they were at loggerheads about something else? What if you were the person whose behaviors de-escalated the tensions by showing that it is possible to have valid differences of opinion and still make great progress?

Let's walk around the **PDCA** cycle again. Imagine you are using the **PDCA** learning circle and climbing the spiral ramp one step at a time for a group project; thus, the outer circle on figure 7.

SHARED PLANNING

In order to have SHARED ACTION, we have to collectively agree on what we want to actually do in SHARED

PLANNNG. Without a clear shared set of specific steps, every SHARED PLAN is doomed. At the greatest extreme, we gather every stakeholder to elicit their key objectives, summarize them into one clear single goal, and build a SHARED PLAN.

This is where we form a hypothesis of exactly what the issue is and how to master it. Good planners are usually convergent thinkers, talented at focus. You can hear them say, "Let's narrow options" to improve focus.

It can be very difficult to get the right people and input into the plan. This calls for the humility to reach out and include those who think our SHARED PLAN should be pointed toward perhaps widely different objectives. It takes considerable leadership skill and sensitivity to successfully navigate in this realm. Absent that skill and step, this exercise would be no different than any other prior attempt.

The challenge will be to come to agreement about a single clear shared mission for this specific project when the number of stakeholders is large and diverse. This is where brain styles will play an important part. Can we pursue our own individual objectives and preferences while collaborating with others to also preserve their individual objectives and preferences?

How do we ensure we are working on the most important thing? This is the essence and challenge of collaboration and leadership. Can we ensure our SHARED PLAN effectively meets the inspirational needs of the front line?

The front line drives the bottom line!
—Unknown

Do we each have to get everything we can ever dream up with this project, or can we use the 80–20 rule to move in the right direction a few steps? People who are good at SHARED PLANNING are usually good at convergent thinking. That is, they can gather key considerations into focus to distill a workable PLAN. In order to do this, they have to limit distractions, usually by ignoring things that are not the root cause of primary importance at this moment (think five whys).

The SHARED PLAN should clearly define project success as its key element. What do we most want as an outcome? Practice your learning and collaboration skills so the needs of others are met.

Unfortunately, when thinking of this critical narrowing of focus, I am reminded of the US Congress. As they fight in circles across party lines, they build huge spending bills. They have to keep adding and adding little side perks in order to maintain support for the entire spending bill. Then many things that have little to do with the primary challenge come along for a free ride. This is terrible strategy for improving focus, learning, accountability, and high performance in the face of the initial challenge.

The other extreme is to allow just one or perhaps just a few brains to define the project's mission and develop a SHARED PLAN to reach that goal. Certainly, this will make it much easier to clarify the mission, thus simplifying the PLAN, but that mission and its impacts may not be well received by those called upon to make it happen.

If a group of people can't get aligned behind the mission, they are less likely to fully invest their energies. This becomes a PLAN SHARED rather than a SHARED PLAN. More, when there is mission confusion, we frequently find, once underway, that many are actually pursuing their own personal missions under the cover of the SHARED PLAN. This is a huge sinkhole open to those who do not fully understand the difference between a truly SHARED PLAN and a PLAN SHARED.

Efficiency is the challenge here. If we have too many brains involved, interaction processes and diversity of style or thought cause chaos and lack of shared alignment. Relying on too few brains tends to lead to narrower definitions and SHARED PLANs that miss the need and fail to inspire those working toward its SHARED PLAN outcome. So the first issue is to get the right people to build the SHARED PLAN.

This a cultural challenge. If trust is high, many will be willing to allow others they trust to point the way with only minor adjustments. If cultural trust is low, few will be willing to just allow others to point the way. This is why a culture of trust plays such a critical role in organizational learning, accountability, and higher levels of performance.

> *Leadership exists when people are*
> *no longer victims of circumstances*
> *but participate in creating new*
> *circumstances. Leadership is*
> *about creating a domain in which*
> *human beings continually deepen*
> *their understanding of reality*
> *and become more capable of*
> *participating in the unfolding of*
> *the world. Ultimately, leadership*
> *is about creating new realities.*
> *—Peter Senge*

It is critical to understand that trust builds slowly over time. It is embedded in the culture. I have heard it described like the water in a fishbowl. The fish does not even know it is there, but it affects everything about how the fish feels and behaves. Trust is built over many replications of working together on things with openness, honesty, and integrity. It can be destroyed by one false move where leaders impose mandates for expediency. Think of your own life and work and how trust plays a part in how easy it is for you to work with others or not.

I tend to think of shared planning like a team building something. They look around for useful resources. They only have what they have available, so they have to be resourceful and creative. Some will be good at thinking up the end product, and some will be better at the actual construction. Some will "lean in," and some will "lean out." The important thing is that they do it together as that builds the shared culture. A way to think of this is to think of a submarine that needs to remodel itself to meet emerging needs while it is at sea and underway. The only talent and resources you have are already on board. The question is what can you do with them?

Culture eats strategy for breakfast.
—Peter Drucker

Anticipate potential organizational barriers and how you will overcome or skirt them. You might want to look up "Premortem." Work to at least include the key diverse stakeholders in the development of the PLAN so they can be invested in the DO, CHECK, and ADJUST phases. If they help build the PLAN, they will help make it happen, work to overcome barriers, and own and defend the results.

Never doubt that a small group
of thoughtful, committed citizens
can change the world;
indeed, it's the only thing that ever has.
—Margaret Mead

The best PLAN in the world will falter if it fails to address the need that drove the whole effort in the first place. A good PLAN only partially performed is better than a perfect PLAN that never gets supported and thus completed and accepted.

We might consider including a broad range of stakeholders or a more limited one, depending on the scope of the project, the likely anticipated impact on others, the inherent risks of the PLAN, and the scope, cost, and duration of the project, etc.

Think about designing a product for sale. Should you just rely on your own knowledge of the market and past consumer preferences, or would it be better to consider the buyers'/users' needs or wants in the design? What about customer preference for things they have yet to know exist? Perhaps you can scare up some dreamers to add zest to your range of options? At a minimum, be sure to include key stakeholders in the PLAN phase. Like many efforts, the level of involvement needed depends on the issue at hand.

I can answer any question in
two words: it depends.
—Anonymous Consultant

Because it does just depend on
everything else ... and mostly
it depends on the culture and
the context of the challenge.

Once you have the right people on the team, make and document a SHARED PLAN that all commit to follow. Many SHARED PLANs fail due to not respecting or meeting this challenge. This is a critical step toward a more disciplined approach. This will be a big part of the eight-step process we are building toward here.

The key words are "commit to." If you don't specifically and overtly ask for commitment, don't just assume you have it. Be very direct in your request for commitment. Ask "Can we count on you for this?" and "What obstacles will you face?" Then work with that information to set a clear, unobstructed path. If you can't come to a PLAN that gets clear and honest commitment, you have failed your role as a leader, and your PLAN will likely fail.

In my leadership development work for the past twenty-five years, I think this paragraph may be the most important takeaway I passed on to my students. Many are too timid to ask for the very thing they need most to ensure team success.

It is unfortunately much too easy to have planning sessions where the most important discussions occur outside at break or after the meeting because full exploration of the issue was not culturally tolerated, safe, or allowed. We have all been to those kinds of meetings. That can't be the norm for a high-performance organization. Talented leaders create the learning environment by their behaviors.

> *Most leadership strategies are*
> *doomed to failure from the outset.*
> *Leaders instigating change are often*
> *like gardeners standing over their*
> *plants, imploring them: "Grow! Try*
> *Harder! You can do it! No gardener*
> *tries to convince a plant to want to*
> *grow. If the seed does not have the*
> *potential to grow, there is nothing*
> *anyone can do to make a difference.*
> —*Peter Senge,* as quoted by Adam Kahane

Sometimes planning meetings evolve to just be the most powerful players driving their own agendas. This leads to failed shared PLANs and rework since real alignment and thus commitment is lacking. Take the time to get deep true full input to get all the dreaded unmentionable issues on the table and addressed. If not, you will find yourself back at the same place in the future wondering what went wrong.

> *If you don't have time to do it right,*
> *when will you have the*
> *time to do it over?*
> —*John Wooden*

An interesting aspect of organizational learning is this challenge of incorporating the right input into the SHARED PLAN. One might say that is also part of the learning. Too few brains, not enough diversity, and the PLAN fails. Too many brains, can't get true and effective narrowed consensus, and the PLAN fails.

The key is the authentic behavior of the leaders. What will they stand for, and what will they stand against in terms of selection and behavior of the participants? The best leaders know their own behaviors will either taint or bless all other aspects of the process. Smart leaders have a "theory of mind" about others in their organizations. You should look theory of mind up on the internet.

Theory of mind refers to the abilities underlying the capacity to reason about one's own and others' mental states. This ability is critical for predicting and making sense of the actions of others, is essential for efficient communication, fosters social learning, and provides the foundation for empathic concern. I think this is key for building trust.

There are many good books on leading change. The issue of how to gather, honor, and manage input to decision-making plays a huge part in collective motivation. I encourage you to explore this subject as a stepping stone to better collective decision-making. See *The Organization of the Future* by Frances Hesselbein et al.

Think of times when you were inspired to work toward goals set by others and times when you were not moved to support a SHARED PLAN, perhaps becoming even a mild saboteur? This is a key realization and learning for leaders. Considering this, we are applying **PDCA** at an even higher level of sophistication. Let's hope we learned from the process!

We usually know who the good planners are. They are convergent thinkers, good at narrowing options to get a workable plan. They stand out. People tend to naturally defer to them when the planning gets complicated. Perhaps we can be good team players and trust in those who are better planners than we are? Remember the 80–20 rule. Get the big ideas right.

If we make and bet on huge long-term complex PLANs, we are unlikely to be fully successful. As an alternative, if we take small incremental steps of testing new ways consistent within one huge, long-term, complex overarching strategy, we are more likely to more efficiently accumulate useful learning and evidence-based outcomes that add up to our overall grand plans.

More simply said, build a set of small discrete projects that can be successful individually. Build them so they add up to our much higher overall goal. Build a chain of small strong links that are each successful. Get good at building and completing small PLANs before building big complex PLANs.

I really like the phrase "hold our plans lightly." The quality of a PLAN is usually tested in the first attempt to implement it. Adaptive management is being ready to revise our PLAN fluidly while still holding on to a clear written PLAN.

> *We are crossing the river*
> *by feeling for stones.*
> *—Deng Xiaoping*

SHARED ACTION

Once we have a SHARED PLAN, we move on to SHARED ACTION. If the SHARED PLAN is good and all the DOers follow it exactly, we will be able to actually find out if the PLAN worked and the hypothesis was correct. Collectively commit in advance to follow the SHARED PLAN exactly to test the hypothesis. Nothing more, nothing less. Refer to figure 7 again. SHARED ACTION is usually dominated by people who are "get-it-done thinkers." They frequently have little patience for the other parts of the **PDCA** cycle. They just want to get moving. You can hear them say, "Quick, let's just do it!"

That said, also commit to return the group to SHARED PLANNING if or when problems emerge in SHARED ACTION. This is the essence of adaptive management. Keep in mind our three key objectives, which are to (1) learn and build capacity, (2) be accountable, and (3) produce great performance. This is a place where brain styles will come into play as individuals act out of their natural tendencies. Some will want to go back to the drawing board; others will object mightily at this delay.

A well-developed co-created SHARED PLAN with buy-in from stakeholders and DOers will work better than ever expected if well performed. The reason is that if all the DOers are deeply committed to the SHARED PLAN, they will move independently and collectively to see it succeed. Even if they are not working in close proximity or directly with each other, each DOer will be moving toward the

SHARED PLAN since they helped build it, and they are deeply invested in its success. They too want it to succeed.

> *I repeat: Never doubt that a small*
> *group of thoughtful, committed,*
> *citizens can change the world. Indeed,*
> *it is the only thing that* ever *has.*
> —*Margaret Mead*

Literally thousands of minor obstacles will emerge in the paths of each of the DOers. If they truly commit to the SHARED PLAN, they will each move to overcome or skirt these local, small, personal, usually unnoticed obstacles by personal initiative in service of the SHARED PLAN and to the others working on it. If they do not fully commit to the SHARED PLAN, literally thousands of similar obstacles will emerge in their paths, stopping progress.

Read the last paragraph again. Yes, go back and read this passage again. Given their lack of full commitment, many obstacles will impede or stop progress. We read these as excuses later when we do a review. But it is critical to recognize they were driven by lack of full commitment at the outset.

One clear symptom of a broken learning cycle is when you find that progress has slowed or stopped relative to the PLAN. Inspection will likely reveal the obstacle was not anticipated in the PLAN, or it may reveal that commitment was lacking, too many other things got in the way. Remember, lack of attention to or unrealistic priorities are unfortunately also part of the actual embedded PLAN, even if they were not identified at the start. This indicates a broken **PDCA** cycle.

Lack of SHARED PLANNING stops SHARED ACTION. Instead of pressing harder for SHARED ACTION, go back to SHARED PLANNING to see what obstacle emerged or what element was missing. Ahhhh, learning!

SHARED REFLECTION

Once the SHARED ACTION phase is complete, it is time to find out if the SHARED PLAN actually worked. Assemble the stakeholders. Do a postmortem (careful review of what actually happened in detail). Think of all the various considerations that went into the SHARED PLAN and assess if the planned steps were actually taken, if objectives were actually and fully met, and what was learned.

The most important thing here is the postmortem needs to be blameless. Think about that and how hard that is to do? People should only be held accountable for their performance commensurate with their experience and training. It is up to the leader to get this right and not expect output beyond the capacity of the people assigned to complete it. Certainly, repeated failures due to lack of attention deserve adjustment. Failures due to the lack of training or capacity accrue to the leader.

The leader must be careful and behave in ways to ensure the focus is on the future, what we learned, and how we can improve. We need to find ways to elevate and celebrate the value of the learning as evidence we are getting collectively and organizationally smarter, and not on making people feel diminished by some outcome beyond their control or capacity.

> *Blame is cheap and fast and easy*
> *and can be fun and reinforcing.*
> *Performance coaching is much harder,*
> *slower, and much more effective.*

Routinely done right, this will change the culture so that the culture embraces learning over knowing. Learning is capacity building for the future. A culture of defending our current knowledge as knowers is a recipe for falling behind.

> *Is changing your mind in*
> *the face of new facts*
> *a weakness or wisdom?*

On figure 7, this is the analysis phase. Go back and study figure 7 again. Be sure to focus on learning to fix the problem and not spend your time trying to fix the blame. Those who are good at SHARED REFLECTION are usually divergent thinkers who want to keep all options open. They are looking for every explanation for success and for places to improve even more.

To the extent the SHARED PLAN was clear and specific with good criteria for judging success, this should be easy. If the PLAN went well, there will be a tendency to skip or skimp on this process. Why not take the time now to ask why this PLAN went well? What capacities did we rely on to explain the success?

Why not find out where we are strong, what we learned, how personal and collective effort was accountable for our collective success, where we could improve even more, and celebrate the great performance? Use every opportunity to celebrate shared success as part of your effort to build a positively reinforcing culture.

This is a great low-cost opportunity to show people you care as much about collective success as you do about failure. This is a chance to celebrate organizational success built on robust solid planning processes and thus planning capacity. This is the key to (1) learning, (2) accountability, and (3) good outcomes. Build a robust tribe of energized learners, learning your way and co-creating a shared successful future.

To the extent the SHARED PLAN was not clear and specific as to what steps were needed and what success would look like, this review will be hard. Hard because not enough was clear. Perhaps the PLAN did not produce the intended outcomes. This is a delicate dance of group dynamics. There will be those who think everything went fine or prefer to avoid the perhaps embarrassing investigation of events and facts. There may be those who think the SHARED PLAN did not meet its objectives, but are hesitant to point to when they or others failed to meet the schedule of the PLAN. Here is the human side of our system speaking to us again.

Truth travels on the highway of trust!

Most of us will have our egos on the defensive for any details that point to us personally being less than perfect. Unfortunately, the path to higher levels of performance is in embracing the very things we can do better next time; thus, the need to embrace that we are not, in fact, perfect.

> *You have to take a risk in order*
> *to leave your current step to*
> *climb to the next step.*
> *—Unknown*

This is why it is so important to define success carefully in advance. This is why leaders need to lead the parade in acknowledging what they could have done differently. It works best if the leader goes first and yet remains open to even more truth about their behavior from others. The leader can show the way. Everyone needs to clearly weigh the truth of the outcome against the PLAN. We are not on a hunt for the guilty; we are on a hunt for the things we could do better next time.

> *Knowers just want to move on.*
> *Learners want to know how to*
> *move on more effectively.*

This is yet another opportunity to surface and learn to rely on the various brain styles in our culture. We can't fix things we can't talk openly about. Avoiding these sometimes painful delicate discussions means we are very likely to just repeat the failings on the next attempt since the real failings are still buried. Leadership behavior becomes critical in handling such interactions. I am again reminded of a quote from my favorite mentor: "The flowers grow best in the shadow of the master." If the leader does it right and shows the way, the rest will follow.

We succeed or fail with the daily cultural practices and behaviors operating in our organization based on the behaviors we routinely exhibit as leaders. And yes, even if your boss can't yet do this, you need to do it as it is the path to your future success despite your boss.

This delicate dance of openness to truth is critical because in order to truly learn from each other, we have to feel free to tell our truths, truths that others may not share or want shared.

The left side of figure 7 shows what happens if we can't talk about what happened realistically. We can't fix things we can't even talk about. This may call for telling others in the group you think they missed the mark, went too far, did not go far enough, missed deadlines, or overspent, etc.

Don't worry they are not listening to you; worry they are watching you.
—Unknown

Others in the group have to feel welcome and empowered to tell you the same while each accepts and embraces that indeed every one of us can always do better, and the receiver of this information has to hear it, and then with good humor and humility, be able to work with it to see what final group assessment can be made. This takes humility, maturity, and authenticity—all part of organizational capacity based on trust. Brain styles need to be respected to ensure all aspects of the issue are considered. The more the culture promotes open productive forward-looking sharing, the more of the problem can be talked about and hopefully addressed.

On figure 7, I call SHARED REFLECTION the Critical Truth Zone. If the members of the group are unwilling or unable to fully express their views of what happened because they feel unsafe or threatened in any way, then the entire effort will stall. If you can't talk about it, you can't fix it!

While we can never share everything, moving toward more deep sharing will move us to talking about and working on a higher percentage of the issues on the human side of the system that are holding us back. This calls for tact and emotional intelligence. These skills improve with practice.

The triangles represent issues or challenges to be considered. The dark-shaded areas are the portion of the issue that for some cultural reason can't be discussed. Perhaps it is the bosses' oft-stated bias or some coworker's sacrosanct domain? If we can't talk about it, we certainly can't fix it. Ask yourself if your organization has issues that suffer from this conundrum.

This is cultural. If the leaders work to improve openness and treat the delayed or poor work and process failures as welcome learning opportunities, then collaboration and group learning can occur. If opinions and truth are suppressed for expediency, power, or safety, then individuals withhold their opinions, and group learning stalls. Then that outcome will overshadow the next attempt at group effort in a downward spiral.

> ***Fear is the dark room where***
> ***negatives are developed.***
> — *Zig Ziglar*

Sometimes we feel we just don't have time to stop and review our work. We just have too much to do. On the other hand, we know there is never enough time to do things right and always enough time to do them over. We are now stuck in the PLAN-DO, PLAN-DO doom loop.

The key is to show by example that every opinion is welcome and honored to the extent it is relevant. Leaders can improve the chances of this by personally inviting everyone to comment. For those who are more reluctant, it will take more time. Be sure your process makes time for those who are usually less talkative.

In my experience, some of the very best ideas came from those who rarely ever voice an opinion. They are observers and can have keen and valuable insights to what is needed. Encourage an open, free-flowing chat that seems to run on too long. That is when some of the best ideas and buried facts emerge. Think of meetings you have been in where topics were discussed quickly and then better ideas emerged at the water cooler after. Once you dedicate time to reviewing a situation, take the time to do it right.

Work to balance input from the more vocal and the less vocal. Use your inquiry skills to ensure all participants are heard and aspects of the issue are explored. This will pay benefits far beyond the current dialogue. With this, you will show that everyone is valued and you are interested in them and their ideas now and in the future. This is chance for the leader to show what learning looks like. This is an opening to demonstrate authentic leadership that is part of "how we work here."

Think on that for a bit and how that affects the success of the organization and everyone in it now and in the future. How good are you at seeking and valuing opinions that differ from your own? What important information or opinion is held by others that you have yet to fully hear, understand, and appreciate?

Does your own brain style get in the way of your own learning? Mine does. What if you could just let go a bit of that certainty in pursuit of shared understanding?

I need to be more open to what I might not yet fully understand.

People good at CHECKing are usually divergent thinkers. They want to go wide and consider all options. They want to be sure nothing was missed. They can be very helpful in finding the leverage points to build new more robust mental models of our systems. They tend to dig deeper and think wider.

CHECKers want to roam all across the landscape and are the opposite of PLANners, who tend to be good at narrowing the range of options to the most important. This sometimes puts the very people we most need to forge a collaborative outcome at odds with each other since they view the world through the lenses of widely different brain styles. We need to acknowledge this reality and work through it. It is something to celebrate, not seek to push under the radar. Talented leaders can point the way by clarifying that both viewpoints are valid, respected, and useful in fully understanding the outcomes.

The main thing is to keep the main thing the main thing!
—Peter Senge

If you have ever had the good fortune of working in a true learning organization culture that valued facts over competing opinions, you will never forget how liberating it felt and will spend your energy trying to recreate it wherever you are.

I read somewhere that decades of psychological research have shown that people heartily embrace congenial nonfacts rather than face difficult and perhaps painful truths. When confronted with disconfirming evidence, people tend to cling to their erroneous but hard-held beliefs. Humans often seek stasis at the expense of progress.

Flashy whoppers spread faster than
complex facts and are remembered
even after being debunked by facts.
Falsehoods fly and truth comes
limping along slowly after it
—attributed to Jonathan Swift
(1667–1745, Ireland)

It can take years to build a learning culture and only a few leader behavioral blunders to stifle it. **PDCA** at the group level, while so valuable, can be hard to build and maintain. It takes a special kind of leader and culture to make this work and continually build it to ever higher rates of organizational effectiveness. The best leaders inspire followers by their behaviors dedicated to shared learning.

The easy way out usually leads
to an even darker future.

SHARED MEANING

Take another look at figure 7. Once the group has come to shared truths about the results of its SHARED ACTION via SHARED REFLECTION, it is time to decide what to do with these new improved mental models. What did we learn as we went around the **PDCA** cycle and stepped up the learning ramp? What newly acquired wisdom can we now use to improve our SHARED PLAN for next time? We want to (1) learn to gain wisdom, (2) operate in accountable ways, and (3) enjoy great performance.

Our newly acquired mental model should make our next SHARED PLAN even more robust. This is the part of the cycle where synthesis occurs. SHARED MEANING calls for the stakeholders to collaborate on what was learned that now can be used in the next plan.

Those good at SHARED MEANING are systems thinkers. You can hear them saying, "Let's find the leverage points." If we can't extract some useful learning for the future, we are just going around in circles, not going up the spiral ramp toward higher levels of future performance and capacity.

Finally, on figure 7, notice the big R+ in the center. This stands for the big doses of positive reinforcement that will be needed on many levels for all this learning to be realized. It is up to the leader to provide the positive reinforcement for the hard work of sharing and learning together.

The simple concept of R+ comes from *Bringing Out the Best in People* by Aubrey C. Daniels, PhD. In order to do this well, the participants need to become more open and more vulnerable to sharing in the critical truth zone, especially when their egos are on the line and it is obvious to everyone they missed some detail or could have performed better. This is where authentic leadership is critical. If the leader's behaviors can't build a culture that supports this, no amount of cajoling will bring about the great results that are possible and now missed.

> *Consider these choices:*
> *Talking at others*
> *Talking to others*
> *Talking with others*
> *Sharing thoughts with others*
> *Sharing thoughts together*
> *Thinking together*
> *Learning together*

This is the fundamental learning cycle applied to teams, groups, and organizations. The issue is, can you get to the planned outcome, useful shared meanings, and incorporate the learnings from that into your next attempt at this or any other challenge? The learnings are there. They always are. You paid for them. Did you get them? Can you make them into useful resources for the next challenge? Can you turn them into new permanent powerful capacities?

PDCA or PDCB, what's it going to be?

Back to brain styles. Some people are exceptionally good at DOing. You see this as their strength. They are the ones you go to when you have to get something important done on time. Others are much better at PLANning. They are the ones you know who always have a plan. They can tell you how it all fits together. They can tell you what resources will be needed. They are the ones you go to when you know you need a detailed plan to ensure steps and resources will all coincide. PLANners rarely forget to ensure needed resources, for example, while others may stumble and fumble when this brain-style deficit surfaces in their work.

Others are best at CHECKing. These are the ones asking sometimes pesky embarrassing questions and comparing notes back to what was planned. They are the ones with the sometimes amazingly painful memories of what was said and planned. They are the ones who will know where the resources went. They are the ones you want on your side when you are trying to hold someone else accountable. Typically, these are the ones with detailed records and project files. They are life's natural CHECKers.

Finally, there are those who are really good at ADJUSTing. These folks are good at taking the PLAN, DO, and CHECK results, drawing out the most important outcomes, synthesizing what worked, what didn't, and what PLAN changes are needed to make to ensure the next attempt will be better. They are the systems thinkers. They are the opposite of DOers. These brains are best at synthesizing the most valuable leverage points to use in the next **PDCA** cycle.

Thus, these different brain styles have to work in concert to (1) learn, (2) hold each other accountable, and (3) perform, gradually raising the collective bar of performance. This only works if we learn to rely on those who have talents and brain styles perhaps much different than our own.

Think about this. If you are hiring a new person for your team, are you more likely to hire someone who challenges you to new heights or hire someone who thinks like you do? What if you eventually hired them all with traits like yours, and the team has little thinking diversity in terms of **PDCA**? Perhaps understanding this way will make you more appreciative of others who challenge your way of thinking.

This is how the use of **PDCA** moves performance up the spiral ramp of capacity. The more a team works together over time, each exercising their best skills, the more effective they can be if they actually recognize and rely on each other's natural talents, and they challenge themselves as a team to get better and better. But only if they learn to lean on each other's strengths and minimize overreliance on their own personal brain styles. This is a huge insight and challenge.

Good things come to those who PDCA!

This challenge exists for the individual and for the organization. As individuals, can we learn to shift mental modes to ensure we take all four **PDCA** steps? In an organization, can we drive to ensure all four ways of looking at some efforts are in use? And then we can practice **PDCA** with discipline to ensure our approach and outcomes promote us to (1) learn, (2) be accountable, and (3) have good outcomes!

Another issue to deal with is the issue of uncertainty in our planning. Clearly every plan is a product of our imperfect understanding of what is going on and why we are getting the results that drives us to make a PLAN to get better at something in the first place.

For example, in a military campaign, we have made some assessment of the enemy's capacities, and we set our PLAN to deal with those. Then once underway, reality strikes. Soldiers learn this as

> *No plan survives contact*
> *with the enemy.*

> *Derived from:*

> *No plan of operations extends with*
> *certainty beyond the first encounter*
> *with the enemy's main strength.*
> *—Helmuth von Moltke,*
> *Prussian General, 1870s*

The fact is, no organization on the face of the planet, in recent times, does more planning than the US military since they know it is the process of planning that builds better understanding and resilience. Think about that for a bit. It is the process of planning more than the PLAN itself that makes us strong.

Disciplined planning challenges us to think more clearly about the resources we have and need. It forces us to think more clearly about what might happen and then, better, what else might happen. Good plans don't consider only one outcome. It might be useful at this point for you to look up Scenario Planning. Think of the thinking behind the thinking that goes into making a good PLAN.

> *Plans are useless. But planning*
> *is indispensable.*
> —*General Dwight D. Eisenhower*

Few reading this will be faced with military planning. Most of us live in a world where there is more time to react to emerging changes, and the consequences of failure are not so severe. Leaders need to chart a course and stick with it most of the time, unless emerging facts show it is too flawed to continue, then re-cycle to shared planning. From that first upsetting outcome, you have learned something valuable, strengthening learning, accountability, and future performance. Celebrate that! You have learned you are not as smart as you thought you were. What a concept! This is a free gift. What a great chance to be more realistic about our learning and our leadership.

The issue is not just how firm or clear your PLAN is. It is equally important to know how much shared commitment there is to make the PLAN happen. All the participants need to be deeply invested in enacting the plan together, sticking to it exactly, and agreeing when to stop and go back and reformulate a better plan, when to use adaptive management.

> *The most powerful tool any soldier*
> *carries is not his weapon but his mind.*
> —*General David Petraeus*

We all face this conundrum every day. When do we stick with the PLAN, and when do we change it? I am arguing for more discipline in planning and the documentation that will lead to actual learning.

> *Have backbone; disagree and commit. Leaders are obligated to respectfully challenge decisions when they disagree, even when doing so is uncomfortable or exhausting. Leaders have conviction and are tenacious. They do not compromise for the sake of social cohesion. Once a decision is determined, they commit wholly.*
> —*Jeff Bezos*

If you are interested in learning more about this train of thinking, I recommend the excellent book *Superforecasting: The Art and Science of Prediction* by Philip E. Tetlock and Dan Gardner.

Another consideration is the arrival of a black swan. Google "What Is a Black Swan?" A black swan is an unpredictable event that is beyond what is normally expected of a situation and has potentially severe consequences. Black swan events are characterized by their extreme rarity, severe impact, and the widespread insistence they were obvious in hindsight.

Sometimes what happened in the past is not a very good predictor of what is coming. Circumstances have changed, and we are faced with some totally new challenge. This book, with its bonus chapter on systems thinking and the eight-step template, is a good start on building organizational resilience in the face of black swans.

Once you decide on a path, you will move to finding out if you and/or the people in your organization can actually do what is needed. This is where the rubber meets the road and where understanding what drives a high-performance culture becomes critical.

Take a careful look at figure 8. It shows the four key steps to performance. It shows what it takes for someone or an entire organization to actually take on a challenge and be successful.

Figure 8

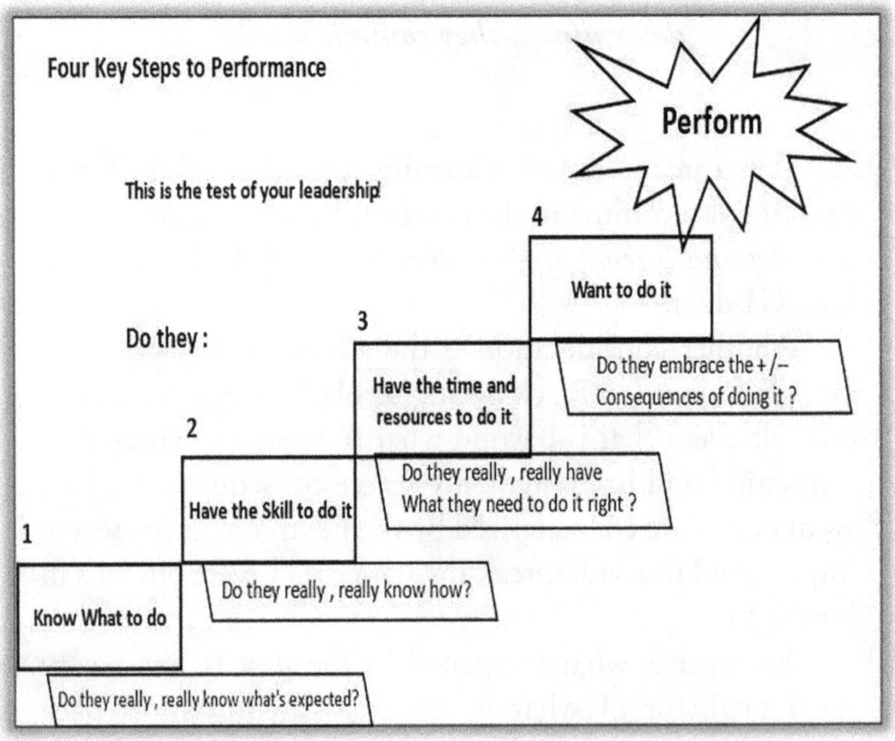

Four Key Steps to Performance

This is the test of your leadership!

4 — Perform — Want to do it — Do they embrace the +/− Consequences of doing it?

Do they:

3 — Have the time and resources to do it — Do they really, really have What they need to do it right?

2 — Have the Skill to do it — Do they really, really know how?

1 — Know What to do — Do they really, really know what's expected?

On its face, this all sounds pretty simple. In the next few figures, I will add more needed detail. In order to be successful, we each need to know exactly what is expected of us. Groups of people, indeed whole organizations, need the same. What needs to be done, exactly? And then, do we actually have adequate skill to do what is needed? Do we have the time and resources? And do we actually want to do it?

Take a look at figure 9 for more detail for knowing what to do. Leaders are clearly responsible for this. Even if a group collectively and creatively decides on the next steps to take, specific and clear understanding of expected actions is critical to success, and the leader is still responsible for the outcomes.

Figure 9

Know What to Do?

High Level : For the Organization ..
    Pursuit of the Mission, Vision, and Values resulting in a clearly defined and understood focus on priorities , and the alignment of the efforts of all Employees

Working Level : For the Person
- Does this person know exactly **what** is to be done ?
- Do they know exactly **where, when , why , how , who, and how much ?**
- Do they understand how this links to other work , things to avoid, obstacles, etc. ?

Areas to Address :
- Link the expected action to the shared vision
- Specific clarity of the action – what does success look like ?
- Appropriate measures
- Coherence with other systems
- Constancy

Take a look at figure 10 for more detail on skill. Leaders are clearly responsible for the skill of their workforce. We need competent people. If we as leaders hire or continue to employee people who can't do what we need, we are not leading, and we justly deserve what we get as a result.

Yes, individuals need to continually build their levels of skill, but the organization's leaders are ultimately responsible if they don't have the right people or they do not have the needed skills. No escaping it, the leader is still responsible.

Figure 10

Have the Skill to Do It ?

High Level : For the Organization ..
The organizations capacity to plan, lead , and safely complete the work within specific work processes .

Working Level : For the Person
- Do they have the HARD [Technical] SKILLS to actually do this task ?
- Do they have the VERY HARD [Social] SKILLS needed ?
- Have they the necessary training and support ?
- Do they fear failure or being judged unfairly and thus delay or resist action ?
- What else might be compromising skill ?

Areas to Address :
- Technical skills
- Social / Interpersonal skills
- Work processes
- Understanding how skills are linked to the vision

Next, take a look at figure 11 for more about having the time and resources needed. When you consider if someone has the time and resources to do something, consider it deeply and from their perspective. Yes, from their perspective.

You may think they have what they need, but if they don't think so, it won't matter what you think. If knowing what to do exactly has been unclear, then time and resources can be compromised due to the lack of clarity. It would be hard to know if you had the time and resources if you were not even sure what you were supposed to do.

Figure 11

Have the Time and Resources to Do It ?

High Level : For the Organization ..
The availability of resources such as time, technology, materials, empowerment

Working Level : For the Person
* Does this person really have the time to do this , given other work ?
* Does this person really have the resources to do this ?
* Do they resist or delay action due to some unforeseen fear ?
* What other obstacles might be limiting effective action ?

Areas to Address :
* Resources : time, materials, cooperation or support
* Authority
* Boundaries , seen and unseen that limit action
* Processes that get in the way
* Elimination/ reduction of fears and obstacles

If you faced a huge backlog list or lists of work to do, you may not think you have the opportunity to effectively work on any of them. What if you fear failure, so you try to work on all of them, and thus, little actually gets completed on any of them? The question of time and resources must be answered from the viewpoint of the performer, not the person giving the direction. If it is not clear, the leader has failed.

Next, take a look at figure 12 for more about the desire to move to action. Leaders can't really directly motivate anyone. If you doubt this, take the time now to go online and study up a bit on motivation. Leaders can and do create the conditions under which people are or are not motivated to work toward the goals of the organization. This is the acid test of leadership. The issue is aligning the hearts and minds so that actions all move the organization toward its intended goals. Everything else is just window dressing in service to this critical need.

Figure 12

Want to Do It ?

High Level : For the Organization ..
The effective use of consequences creating a "want to" rather than
a "have to " work environment

Working Level : For the Person
- Does this person really want to do this ?
  if not , do you know why ?
- What unseen obstacles may keep them from doing their best ?
- How might mgmt. actions [yours and others] [now and in the past]
  have contributed to this lack of motivation ?

Areas to Address :
- Clear directions
- Related behaviors
- Feedback History and trust
- Consequences

We individuals always do what we think is best given the circumstances as we perceive them. Leadership behaviors write the script and the score, and then wait to see how it all comes out. We frequently find people who just do what they think is best despite clear directions from others. This is the human side of the system.

Ask yourself who is responsible if key factors in performance are weak or missing.

Take a look at figure 13. It clarifies that we tend to blame performance issues on motivation when the real culprit is mostly failings of direction.

Figure 13

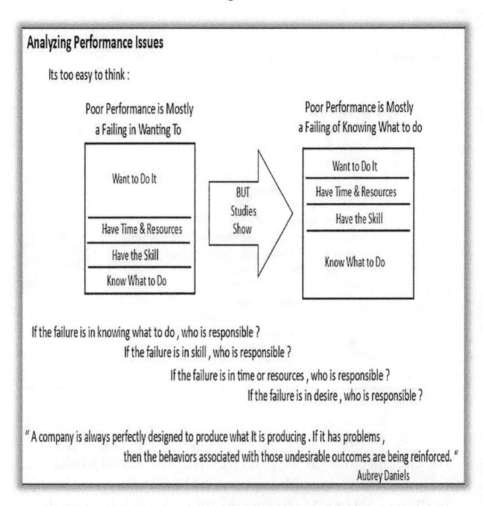

Analyzing Performance Issues

Its too easy to think :

Poor Performance is Mostly a Failing in Wanting To

Want to Do It

Have Time & Resources

Have the Skill

Know What to Do

BUT Studies Show

Poor Performance is Mostly a Failing of Knowing What to do

Want to Do It

Have Time & Resources

Have the Skill

Know What to Do

If the failure is in knowing what to do , who is responsible ?

If the failure is in skill , who is responsible ?

If the failure is in time or resources , who is responsible ?

If the failure is in desire , who is responsible ?

" A company is always perfectly designed to produce what It is producing . If it has problems , then the behaviors associated with those undesirable outcomes are being reinforced. "

Aubrey Daniels

People want to be inspired by the behaviors of their leaders to work on worthy projects that make them feel competent and honored for their part in the success.

Stop! Now go back and review the past few figures again. Yes, review the charts again as these are very important to understand. These simple ideas are key to success on your journey to learning, accountability, and performance.

Figure 14 shows the impact of weak leadership behaviors on performance.

Figure 14

Effect of Weak Leadership		
If Key Factors are Ignored		
Ignored	**Personal Outcome**	**Organizational Outcome**
Know What to do ?	Confusion , Everyone working what they think is most important	No alignment of Efforts , Confusion, Chaos , Poor outcomes
Skill to do it ?	Wasted time, errors , re work accidents , poor quality	Accumulated inefficiency Creates persistent drag on success
Have the Time and Resources ?	Frustration, slow down, competition for priorities or resources	Fail to meet objectives Turnover do to frustration
Want to do it ?	Inaction, look around and wait for others	Unmotivated work force fails to meet objectives compromising success

Want to do it is largely dependent on the first three
and the last one to address once the others are satisfied

Given our natural self-centered human natures, it is so easy to always assume things go haywire because others just aren't motivated. What conditions might exist that would explain that lack of motivation? What might you have done or not done that is contributing to the lack of drive to want to do what is needed? Consider carefully the bold statement on the bottom of the figure. Now let's move on.

Are you always motivated? What kinds of leadership failures do you experience from others that mess with your own drive to do what is needed? Our organizations are full of good, well-intentioned people, just like you. What might be in their way of great performance? What leadership behaviors might be the roadblock to much higher levels of learning, accountability, and performance? Do your behaviors create roadblocks to others that hold the whole group back?

Appendix C is a two-page assessment tool for you to help determine how well you are doing at leading others.

Now let's move on to some ways of thinking about when to make changes in search of better outcomes and when to stick with proven process to capture the efficiency of routine processes repeated with precision. We need a criteria for making such decisions. Lack of focus in this area can lead us to be trying to fix everything at the same time, which usually leads to the scattering of effective resources and nothing getting fixed.

Chapter Summary

This chapter expanded the **PDCA** foundation for individuals to the fundamental learning cycle for groups and how it is used to improve organizations and processes over time. Now we will turn our attention to sharing a bit about how to focus our attention on the most important issues for improved efficiency in learning, accountability, and performance.

CHAPTER 4

───── ✑ ─────

Routines for Efficiency vs. Trying New Ways: How Much of Each?

Chapter Summary

This chapter speaks to the issue of when to take on working to improve something and when to leave it alone in favor of working on something else. This can be a critical decision for leaders as resources are scarce and need to be directed to those areas of greatest leverage for learning, accountability, and performance.

If you always do what you always did,
You will always get what
you always got.
If you want to get what you never got,
You have to do what you never did.
—Unknown

111

Perhaps you have heard this before. While it is not always true, it is largely true. If you want a new or better outcome, you will probably have to do something new and different.

> *What got you here won't get you there.*
> *—Marshall Goldsmith*

Yet to be most efficient, most people generally believe the best path is to diligently and rapidly repeat the same standard process, sometimes called best practice, over and over again without variation. In fact, that is the mantra for efficiency.

On the other hand, if you want to be more effective, you have to be ready to adjust rapidly to emerging conditions, to learn, to adapt! Some people call this adaptive management. This is a dilemma. How can someone dedicated to the efficiency of holding things routinely constant ever learn new improved ways without trying them?

> *Step through new doors.*
> *The majority of the time there's*
> *something fantastic on the other side.*
> *—Oprah Winfrey*

The key is to hold most things steady and carefully change only a few things at a time, measuring carefully for emerging changes (positive or negative) in outcome.

The eight-step process template coming in the next chapter addresses this dilemma by carefully selecting the most likely path to improvement and then making and then fully implementing a good specific PLAN well, without changing it while underway. Then using the measured results for better or worse, taking the learnings from that PLAN and ADJUSTing the next PLAN. So we try to do everything according to PLAN, both the routine for efficiency and the nonroutine for learning.

This calls for discipline since at the first hiccup, it is very enticing to modify or abandon the PLAN on the fly once under way. Every time we change the PLAN, or worse abandon it, we lose the chance to learn if it would have delivered the intended results if left unchanged. We miss the opportunity to learn about what PLAN works and perhaps what won't. Additionally then, the initial PLAN is no longer in play; so technically, we now don't even have a PLAN.

Old Thomas Edison's story is ubiquitous. He tried ten thousand light bulb filaments till he found the one that worked, and the rest is history. He had to know what did not work so he did not repeat that trial again. We are usually so driven by the goal to finish something and stay moving in the right direction that the completion drive in us far overshadows the goal of learning what actually worked or didn't to bring about the final result.

See figure 15. Routine processes are valuable in that they are most efficient. Organizations need efficient operations to survive or thrive. No one should be or can be changing everything at the same time (although sometimes that is what it feels like). And yet they also need to change to adapt to new challenges.

The gray area of the chart shows we should hold most efforts to standard methods. The white area shows we should also be steadily trying to improve on carefully selected issues. We need to have some clear guidance for when to hold to repeating best practices and when to try new things. Interestingly, if you are highly efficient doing the wrong things, the wronger you become.

Some portion of our time needs to be dedicated to trying new things. This is the argument for "Beta Tests" of new processes. A beta test takes a proposed new way of proceeding and puts it to the test in some specific and usually limited way to see if it actually does produce the intended outcomes. So we do actually do get something from them, even if they fail to deliver the intended results, as long as we can identify the learnings. The worst outcome is to abandon the effort and never even get the learnings.

Figure 15

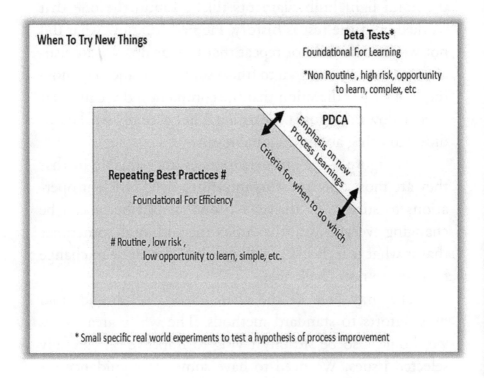

*Not all intended consequences
of our actions materialize, but
all the unintended do.*
—*Dee Hock, Visa International*

The eight-step template sets a CASA pattern for beta tests. Each test is intended to be discrete and focused on testing only a few proposed improvements at a time.

Sometimes we do not get a benefit from our test, and we consume attention and resources in the process. I guess that would be an argument for never trying anything new. Beta tests, if conducted carefully using **PDCA**, can substantially add to our capacity—capacity for learning, accountability, and performance. Think of it like a gym membership for your brain.

As each test comes to a close, if there are valuable improvements, they are merged into the next PLAN. If not, other things can be tried on the next iteration. At least we know one more thing that does not work.

This is an argument for not building huge complex PLANs. Rather, take well-laid-out small specified steps toward your goal. This is frequently called shaping, successive approximations toward the goal, or continuous process improvement. I urge you to look these up for deeper and richer understanding.

We want to be efficient about most things. And yet we want to be able to test new ideas as well in pursuit of effectiveness. We need to be clear about which of these is in play in each part of our work. Think about the four key steps to performance in the last chapter. Be sure the people doing the work know the difference between following routine procedures well for efficiency and trying new things for learning.

The decision to repeat a standard practice or make a beta test of a new practice needs to be a well-communicated conscious choice. We don't want our workers to be confused about the exact methods they should be using on any one project. Otherwise, driven by laudable motives, they will be making steady changes to be more productive as they see it. This is why outdated procedure manuals fill dusty shelves and have little connection to what is actually being done, and it is why prior learnings are ignored and disasters are repeated. Let's hope your airline pilot does not make this same mistake on your next flight.

I think we could rely on the Pareto Principle for deciding. I think perhaps 80 percent of our work should be held constant for efficiency purposes, and no more than 20 percent should fall into the beta test category. But this is highly dependent on the nature of the work you are trying to do. If you are not familiar with the Pareto Principle, go look it up now.

Your people need to understand this way of thinking. They need to know they are expected to adhere to well-developed best practices in order to support the organization's mission of learning, accountability, and performance.

If testing is planned, then make it a real test and actually carefully measure the outcomes so you know, not just guess, if it worked. Pre-PLAN to gather actual performance data, and then measure outcomes. There are two whole chapters coming on measurement. Make and test a PLAN.

If the decision is to use a standard practice, then do that well with CASA discipline and avoid the expense and delay of a beta test in favor of the efficiency. Know which game you are playing. See figure 16.

This is an example for an organization that does native habitat restoration work. There are a number of things they do that need to be done efficiently, with no time to waste. These are shown on the left. On the other hand, there are things they do that need to be tested to see how they can be improved; these are shown on the right. It is helpful to create a similar working list for your work. The leadership challenge is to make this process visible. Don't just leave this chance.

Once a decision is made as to which game we are playing, repeat best practices or try a beta test, we need to be disciplined in how we work. We can say repeating standard practice is a PLAN, a PLAN to carefully just follow our best practice with discipline. It's just not a beta test this time so hold all efforts to the standard way. All of those involved need to know which game we are playing this time with this procedure.

PLANs that are not followed are not really PLANs at all. They are wishful thinking. Remember, hope is neither a strategy nor a PLAN. The key is to focus on both the learning and the results that emerge from our well-planned efforts, not to just focus on the results. Our efforts may or may not be effective. We need to learn if they are or not. We will say more about this later when we get to measurement.

Figure 16

Criteria .. For When to do Which .. Best Practices vs. Beta Tests		
REPEAT	**J**	**TRY**
BEST MANAGEMENT PRACTICES		**BETA TESTS**
USE MORE WHEN :	**U**	**USE MORE WHEN :**
ROUTINE WORK		NON ROUTINE WORK
FEW UNKNOWNS	**D**	MORE UNKNOWNS
PREDICTABLE RESULTS		MANY POSSIBLE RESULTS
LOW RISK	**G**	HIGH RISK
SIMPLE TASKS		COMPLEX TASKS
FEW INTERACTIONS	**E**	COMPLEX INTERACTIONS
Examples:		**Examples :**
Moving gravel	**M**	Planning projects
Spraying weeds		Evaluating process failures
Grading to specs	**E**	Testing new theories
Planting trees		Resources are limited
Irrigation system install	**N**	Decision makers are in conflict
Estimating simple jobs		Challenge is unfamiliar
Resources are adequate	**T**	Prior attempts failed
Decision makers agree		Selecting plant species
Challenge is familiar		There is disagreement on theory
Prior attempts succeeded		Sponsor does not accept BMP

I have developed a real aversion to the phrase "we are working on it." What the heck does that mean? I want to hear, "We are on schedule with our PLAN, and we are learning if it will produce the outcome we seek." I love the time-honored phrase "plan the work, and work the plan." That is a statement that exhibits the CASA discipline that leads to learning, accountability, and performance.

You can create a chart similar to figure 16 for your own work processes. The dialogue you will need to get something written down and accepted will be very valuable. It is the group learning from sharing ideas that is most valuable. The chart is only secondary.

This process will help focus your group or team and improve the chances they will stay focused on sticking to PLANs, whether standard practice or beta tests. Usually there is no clear dividing line between the two, so everyone is burning through resources trying to improve everything at once.

Chapter Summary

This chapter discussed the challenge of when to take on working to improve something and when to leave it alone in favor of working on something more critical to learning, accountability, and performance. This can be a critical decision and skill for leaders. It is much too easy to see issues and try to fix them, diluting our capacity to work on the most critical, when some issues do not deserve our attention YET.

Now let's move on to better understanding of how to actually use **PDCA** to pursue our learning, accountability, and performance using the eight-step template.

CHAPTER 5

———— ❧ ————

PDCA: Eight-Step Template for Learning, Accountability, and Performance

Chapter Summary

This chapter expands the basic four-step **PDCA** foundation for individuals and groups to the eight-step template. Built on the fundamental learning cycle, the eight-step template provides a reliable and effective road map for learning, accountability, and performance.

While **PDCA** only has four steps, I have found a consistent and expanded eight-step process template provides needed detail for more effective implementation. While eight steps sound harder to remember, they are actually easier to implement successfully and less open to variance when being applied.

We need to expand the four steps to eight in order to get enough granularity to stay on track. Others have pitched more or fewer than eight steps. No matter; success-ful practitioners involved in Adaptive Management and similar systems thinking process models have a multistep circular process based on **PDCA**. The key element is the circular nature of the process.

This chapter will outline the eight-step process at a high level. Then the next few chapters will go deeper into each step with deeper explanations and linkages to all the rest. It is important to know that each step is taken in sequence, each building on the ones that went before.

Certainly, as we move into this, you will feel these are all familiar terms, ideas, and processes. The prize is when they are assembled and practiced in a disciplined, consis-tent, and systematic set of routine behaviors (Consistent And Systematic Application or CASA). My goal is to make the eight steps easy to understand, connect, and remember in a flowing circular model of how to proceed. Once you see how it all works, it will be quite easy to remember the eight steps since they logically flow one to the next.

Now, finally, here are the eight steps of the template in order.

1. Mission
2. Vision
3. Values
4. Strategy
5. Tactics
6. Measure
7. Learning
8. Next (on to the next iteration or mission)

Some of these are quite detailed, and some are quite simple. None should be new to you. This chapter is to chart out the course for following the eight-step template.

Here is a road map for the next few chapters:

Chapter	PDCA		The 8 Steps
6	PLAN	=	1) Mission 2) Vision 3) Values 4) Strategy
7	DO	=	5. Tactics
8	DO	=	6. Measure—General Overview
9	DO	=	6. Measure—Specific Examples
10	CHECK	=	7. Learning
11	ADJUST	=	8. Next

First, we will turn our attention to how these eight steps fit together into a high-performing cycle of learning, accountability, and performance.

Here is a sports related analogy for the eight steps that may be helpful:

1. **Mission** = the specific game we are playing this time, not some other game or many games; just this one specific game—be specific.

2. **Vision** = the inspiring image of future victory; state what success will look like exactly in three to five appropriate periods; stated in past tense.

3. **Values** = our best intentions and the behavioral rules we will play by for this specific game.

4. **Strategy** = our high-level game plan; key short high-level list only; if these won't do it, we don't have an effective strategy.

5. **Tactics** = our specific roles and actions as individuals; there are usually multiple tactics within/for each strategy item; for accountability, there should only be one named process owner for each tactic.

6. **Measures** = the tally of our individual actions/results for each tactic and the total score; best to have both leading and lagging measures at each level.

7. **Learning** = comes from post-play, quarter, and game reviews of plays, metrics, and final outcomes; what did we learn to use in our next game?

8. **Next** = Let's be sure our recent learnings are incorporated in to our next plan. We are now more capable to play the next game, whatever it is.

Think of how you learned to ride a bicycle or some other activity. You wanted to do it, you planned to do it, you tried, you failed, you thought of what you could do better next time, you tried again and again, till it became second nature.

Now please take some time to study Figure 17. There are some embedded ideas in the text that I won't speak about right now, but will likely resonate with you as you digest this road map.

Figure 17

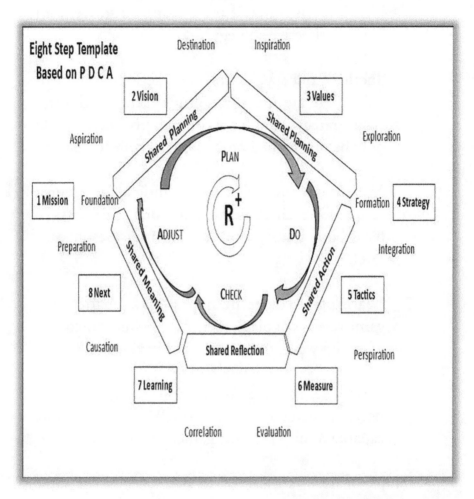

The process begins on the far left at step 1 with Mission and travels clockwise around the diagram back to Mission. Please locate the text below on figure 17. Take the time to think through each step leading to the next step.

1 <u>Mission</u>, 2 <u>Vision</u>, 3 <u>Values</u>, and 4 <u>Strategy</u> comprise the **PLAN** in a group **PDCA**

5 <u>Tactics</u> and 6 <u>Measure</u>

comprise the **DO** in a group **PDCA**

7 <u>Learning</u>

comprises the **CHECK** in **PDCA**

8) <u>Next</u> is the **ADJUST** in **PDCA**

I have chosen to use a group learning approach diagram because the concepts are the same for an individual, but most work is done by groups.

PLAN—The Zone of Shared Planning: Mission, Vision, Values, and Strategy

Consider the descriptor words in the background as added explanation for the mindset of the participants and the process step you are reading about.

1. **Mission (Foundation).** The mission is the reason the team, group, or the project or the effort exists. It is foundational. It is what the entire rest of the effort stands on. If there is no clear mission, then no one will know or care when, how, why, or if it is achieved. The mission is the high-level simple purpose of this effort. And it is a rallying flag for building and holding the commitment of stakeholders.

2. **Vision (Aspiration and Destination).** The vision is the desired destination. It is where the person or group aspire to go with this effort, project, or

---

even an organization. It is the intended outcome. It should be a stretch to achieve, yet a realistic goal given our capacity. Good visions are aspirational in nature. They inspire us to work hard to bring them to fruition because they inspire us to do our best work.

No matter the size of the effort, a vision is critical. If you don't know where you want to go, then any road will take you there, and you will never know when you've arrived. Visions need to be stated as if they have already been attained (use the past tense as if they already occurred. This will matter later when we get to metrics).

3. **Values (Inspiration).** Values are the way we want to focus and interact while working on this effort and the big drivers for those behaviors. They are the things we most need to care about, and they are our principles of conduct. They define our culture.

The values should be an expression of our organization's values as they relate to this specific project. They can be general or specific. They can be deep or surface process statements. They will likely be different and tailored for each project. The key is to clearly state what approach, focus, and behavioral guidance are most needed to commit to when working on this particular effort.

What really matters to you? Your values are an activating intelligence in your life, guiding you toward

*the noble tasks that are yours alone
to do. There are moments in all of
our lives that reveal these values.
Their significance lies not only in
what meaning we make
of them, but also
what we allow those
moments to make of us.*
—*Dawna Markova*

For example, sometimes the most important value for a project is cost control. Another time, the most important is not cost but accuracy. Another project might most need rapid implementation. These are the kinds of clear practical hard values that help set a project in motion toward success.

Softer (actually very hard) values like cooperation, broad inclusion of stakeholders, or happy customers are important, but perhaps sometimes not as much as cost, accuracy, or time. Good values statements are usually a short blend of both hard values like cost, plus some very hard values like trust and teamwork.

Values matter more on group projects as they need to be shared and codeveloped and held in common with others working on this effort. They are still important on projects performed by an individual. Values are formative. Once clearly stated, they can actually help you stay focused and achieve them. I think of them as guardrails for our work. When faced with some dilemma, consulting the projects' values can help sort out the best direction.

> *Your beliefs become your thoughts.*
> *Your thoughts become your words.*
> *Your words become your actions.*
> *Your actions become your habits.*
> *Your habits become your values.*
> *Your values become your destiny.*
> —*Mahatma Gandhi*

If you have clearly stated values and can practice project effort with high ideals, you can improve the culture, the profile of group learning, accountability, the performance outcomes, and group capacity for the next challenge. This is capacity building at its best. Values are where effective interaction skills and respecting alternative brain styles really come into play.

4. **Strategy (Exploration and Formation).** Strategy is naming what high-level general direction and major steps will be taken to meet the objectives of the mission, vision, and values. It will take into account resources, obstacles, resistance, prior and current situations, need for cooperation by others, etc. It is the logical outcome flowing from our intentions developed in the mission, vision, and values. It is the path forward.

   By stating one strategy, we are setting the project approach and thus leaving out many other possible ways of proceeding. Strategy is part of PLAN. A strategy should have only one person responsible for its outcomes at the highest level. Others should report to this person for specific tactics. This is critical for accountability, one of our key goals.

If everyone is accountable, then no one is accountable. You have been to that circus before, over and over, when the post-project failure fingers of blame start pointing out in all directions. We need to build accountability into the PLAN. One person should feel the heat if progress slips for their specific part of the PLAN. They can then make sure the PLAN stays on track.

At a high level, the strategy has to name a fairly high-level short list of activities that will bring about the desired results outlined in the mission, vision, and values. Quality strategies are at best the work of a number of diverse brains focused on pursuing the stated shared objective with a robust **PDCA** orientation. Individuals have to have well-developed effective strategies when working alone as well. A good strategy brings alignment.

Many like to talk strategy, yet few are actually good at it since it is the well-aligned shared intentions and mental models of the performers that make it successful, not some list or chart on a page in a binder. Strategy is making explicit the deep thinking behind our surface thinking on how to proceed. This is not something most of us has experience with or discipline for. Think about it, if everyone already deeply agrees and is aligned on what needs to be done, there would be little need for a written strategy. But we know that is rarely the case.

Humans need to be more specific in laying out plans. Mere words are feeble carriers of complex ideas. There are many good books on the subject. I recommend you study the strategy chapter of the book *Execution* by Larry Bossidy and Ram Charan. The strategy is not a set of detailed action plans; those come next in tactics.

Mission, vision, values, and strategy are considered hard skills. Most people are familiar with these terms as they have been popular jargon words in the past several decades in all walks of life and work. This shows how much **PDCA** has subtly worked its way into our collective consciousness, even if we don't fully recognize or value it.

The early part of the cycle is the most critical to be well developed and is most often the most ignored in favor of getting started immediately. We are usually most intent on action, employing the skills we have had more training and experience in so we can get back to our comfort zone.

It is nearly impossible to solve a problem or capture some opportunity if you can't all closely agree on what the problem or opportunity actually is. If the mission, vision, values, and strategy are wrong, then everything that follows will be wrong. There will be much more to say about mission, vision, values, and strategy in chapter 6.

These first four steps are the product of individuals or more likely groups collaborating and coming up with a set of clear compelling written statements that align their hearts and minds. Notice that mission, vision, values, and strategy fill a large part of the diagram. This is very intentional in that they are foundational.

They do take up all the early time in the project. If they are not well developed, then all that follows will be compromised. Many are so conditioned to just get started with the DOing, they can't really appreciate that they have likely failed to clearly define the very things they need to succeed.

The way team members interact with each other exposes the real actual lived values the individuals and group exhibit in their everyday behaviors. In the mission, vision, and values steps, the prevailing culture will limit or liberate the creativity, stretch, collaboration, and outcome of the entire PLAN.

The PLAN is much less important than the dialogue among a group that leads to the PLAN. If the dialogue is open, rich, and forward-looking, the PLAN will be as well.

The more aligned the hearts and minds are, the less well-documented the PLAN has to be. If the dialogue is fraught with stress, lack of clarity or truth, or stifling, the entire PLAN and its implementation will certainly suffer.

We must talk about our
differences—till our differences
don't make any difference.
—Unknown

Think about it, if everyone deeply shared the identical mission, vision, and values, you wouldn't even need any discussion or rules, and the strategy could be very simple since everyone would be trying to get to exactly the same place the exact same way.

DO = The Zone of Shared Action: Tactics and Measures

Most of us are more familiar and comfortable with the steps in the formation of tactics than any of the other steps. These are considered technical hard skills. These are the kinds of things people take classes for in project management. Please return to figure 17. We need to be competent in this area. I think this is always the area where individuals and teams most need help with metrics.

5. **Tactics (Integration and Perspiration).** Tactics are the specific tasks needed to move forward on the strategy. Tactics are detailed. They are specific. To be effective, they each have a named specific one-person process owner who is accountable for this specific tactic/task in order to build in accountability at every step. They also show clearly what will be done by whom and when, only at a much more detailed level. They translate the higher-level strategy into specific operational activities; all of which need to be completed to make the strategy a success.

   Tactics are the work people do every day on the project. They are the subject of project management approaches and tools. Typically, there is at least one and usually a number of tactics for each element of this particular strategy. They are the DO in **PDCA.** Some should be measured and, collectively, when completed, then unfold to meet the challenge of the strategy.

6. **Measure (Evaluation).** Measure is how we know if we are making any progress on the specific tactics of the strategy. Measurement is part of DO in support of the tactics and strategy. Without measures, how will we know if the PLAN is working? We need measures for most specific tactics. Collectively, the measures for each tactic add up to a measure of the strategy and the PLAN.

   Without measures, we might as well not bother to write a PLAN. Facts based on evidence help guide us forward with clarity. We need to make decisions based on facts, measured evidence, and not opinions. There will be more to say about tactics and measure to come. Just remember, you heard it here first, facts are our friends!

CHECK—The Zone of Shared Reflection: Learning

7. **Learning (Correlation and Causation).** Many leaders or groups struggle to even include CHECK time or processes in their plans and work. If you don't set aside time to CHECK, then you have just planned to have a broken **PDCA** cycle. You might as well just go back to repeating PLAN-DO,

PLAN-DO. In systems thinking parlance, this is called the doom loop.

One effective way to assess the skills of a leader is to just ask to see the PLAN, and then CHECK to see if it has CHECK and ADJUST steps built in and in use. If not, you know this leader fails to understand how processes are improved.

As an individual, do you schedule time mid project to assess how well your PLAN is working? As a leader, do you schedule group time for the same purpose? For example, if you hold meetings and then never stop at the end of the meeting and leave quality time to reflect on what made the meeting useful and what could be improved next time, you are stuck in the doom loop.

Just what did we learn from the preceding steps? How well did we evaluate the results obtained compared to the PLAN? Did we rely on measured facts to determine what worked, or are we still drowning in opinions?

What can we use from the resulting outcomes, good or bad, to make us smarter as we approach the next iteration on this project or on the next challenge we face? If we can't identify what we can do better, then we are stuck at this level of performance. We have stopped ascending the spiral ramp of learning. If you always do what you always did, you will always get what you always got. Perhaps your competitors (individuals or organizations) have mastered this skill while you continue to flounder in the doom loop.

Learning is hard since we have to identify, accept, and embrace where we were clearly not up to the task we started or we failed to take into account important elements in the PLAN. This is where group learning styles really matter. It is hard enough for a single person to acknowledge failings to themselves. It is much harder for a group to manage this since individual and collective failings become more public.

This is where brain styles and the cultural behaviors of the leaders become critical. Learning is considered a very hard skill. It takes courage, persistence, honesty, humility, tact, and compassion. These are the skills of accomplished leaders. These skills set the tone for a culture of learning or not. We want to be learners, not knowers!

ADJUST—The Zone of Shared Meaning: Next

8. **Next (Preparation).** Here is where we ask the "so what" questions. How are we going to actually and fully incorporate the learnings from step 7 in our future work? We did the work and considered the results. So what? Be explicit. What is next? What process or system improvements will we make? How will our learning make us better next time? What would an outsider be able to observe that is new and different in our next attempt? This is where we translate learnings into useful future action.

We paid dearly for this activity and the lessons it holds; how are we going to extract its maximum value for this project or effort and for our overall capacity to meet future challenges? This is where broken **PDCA** cycles go to die. If there is nothing new to try, we are stuck in the doom loop going around and around in a fog to nowhere. Unfortunately, there is a tendency to then turn our talk to self-congratulatory sharing of how hard we worked stories rather than focus on how much smarter we now work.

> *Unless you are learning faster than your competition, the end is in sight.*
> *—Unknown*

Unfortunately, many of us get so much positive reinforcement from our own sense of individual progress or that of our organizations for what we DO, we rarely fully appreciate the critical nature of the **P** in **PDCA.** And we are in such a hurry to get even more kudos for DOing that we minimize any CHECKing and ADJUSTing. We DO the work and take what we get without fully capturing the value from the CHECKing, learning, and ADJUSTing. This is just ignoring the potential capacity building we already paid for.

Now a More Linear Model: The Eight Step Template

Please take some time to study figure 18. This chart is a more linear road map for the same previous circular eight-step process. I urge you to take the time to consider the chart details to see how this all fits together and flows from left to right and also around and back to the beginning. Note that this shows the accumulating knowledge and wisdom being changed by the prior seven steps. If you get good at this, you will begin to remember the eight steps as **M V V S T M L N** as I do. That acronym will make it easy to apply this to whatever you are working on. And I have learned this is a very valuable tool for any and all projects or challenges, large or small.

Figure 18

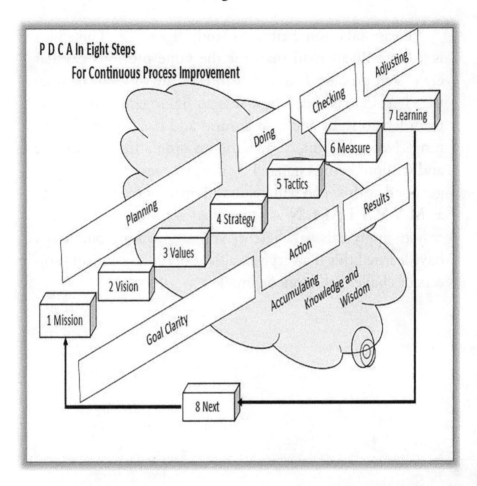

I show this as an ascending staircase as each step leads to a clearer, more effective approach to the challenge of the next step. But note that unless you connect the later steps back to the Next approach so the feedback learning can be incorporated, the value will be lost.

If we did the work and then failed to capture the learnings as part of our new higher level of capacity in our body of knowledge, we wasted some of our effort. We want to (1) learn how to meet this challenge, (2) be accountable for our actions, and (3) perform well on our mission for this challenge. We can apply these eight steps to most everything we do. Certainly, not every challenge needs this approach. But to the extent we can individually and collectively follow a routine template everyone understands, the more efficient and effective our routine behaviors become.

On figure 18, the first four steps of mission, vision, values, and strategy are all about goal clarity, tactics and measure are all about action, and learning is all about results. We pile up accumulating knowledge and wisdom to be re-cycled back through the eight steps so the whole system is changed and elevated by each pass through the cycle.

Now take a look at figure 19. The treasure chest is our accumulated knowledge and wisdom. This can be our core competency. This can be our competitive advantage. This can be our special secret sauce. This can be our differentiation strategy. We can continue to advance and be better than our competition if we know how to accelerate our rate of learning, accountability, and performance.

Figure 19

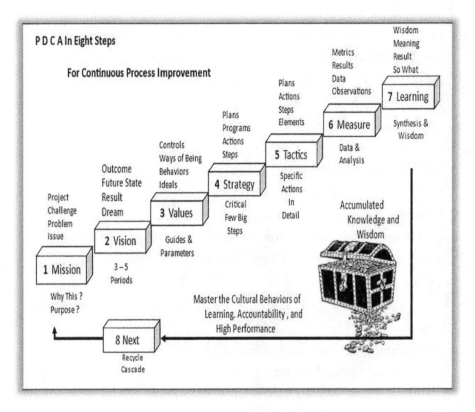

I use a specific set of words in each box to describe the steps. You may prefer or use other words to describe the same or similar ideas. Let's not get bogged down in semantics or terminology. Above each of my steps, I have added some alternative words that you may find more familiar or useful to describe the steps. No matter, but within the system you are using, be sure everyone is using the same terms for the same things. This is much harder than it seems. A chart like this will help.

If you adopt one set of descriptors for the eight steps and gradually institutionalize their use, eventually, everyone will gradually get aligned, confusion will be reduced, and dialogue will get easier and become more time effective. New arrivals will quickly adopt the terminology you select, and it will eventually become the common lexicon of the entire organization—a very useful outcome.

The big challenge is to assemble the steps in a tight formation flowing from the beginning back around to the beginning in the grand circle of **PDCA** and apply it consistently and systematically (CASA). This is the systems thinking approach that incorporates the critical feedback for continuous process improvement.

Under each of the step boxes, I have included clarifying words to help a team create the needed shared statements. Everyone needs to agree on these, or you are already doomed.

For example, under

1) Mission, I have added "Why this?" "Purpose?" The Mission should answer this question in very simple terms; one phrase or a sentence is best.

2) Vision, I use "3 to 5 Periods." I have found defining the Vision in terms of a future time window range very helpful. Each project is different. I use 3 to 5 to mean three to five days, weeks, months, years, or decades, whichever is most applicable. This sets a future time window for the Vision to define for this specific project. Choose what is most appropriate for this challenge, and it does not have to be 3 to 5. Just clearly state the end point. I usually

argue for nearer than farther end points. Name one date. Use 3 to 5 thinking to help select what that date needs to be. Visions should be stated as past tense; in other words, as if they have already been accomplished.

3) Values, I use "Guides and Parameters." The Values should set these for this specific project. We covered this a bit earlier in the text.

4) Strategy, I use "Critical Few Big Steps." The Strategy should be simple to understand, showing the big steps only. Some people call this an elevator speech; that is to say, you could easily outline what you plan to do in the less than two minutes of an elevator ride in a tall building. If you can't chunk it down to this, you do not have a firm grasp on the big changes that will be necessary.

5) Tactics, I use "Specific Actions in Detail." This is where the actual work gets defined and assigned in detail. This is where the work is done. Each tactic should have one, and only one, specific process owner, and it should tell briefly and clearly who will do what by when (WWDWBW).

6) Measure, I use "Data and Analysis." This is where the tactics and results get measured. This is where the facts come from that drive data-driven improvement. Notice I did not include the idea of an opinion.

7) Learning, I use "Synthesis and Wisdom." This is where we take the measures or our results and use that evidence to become smarter so we can improve our process.

8) Next, I show "Re-cycle Cascade." This means we use what we learned in step 7 to cascade to applicable ways to become more effective in our next attempts. Those might be on the same project or on some next project. If we practice these steps with CASA, we will gradually get better and better at working together to overcome obstacles and bring success.

Someday perhaps these eight steps will be as easy to remember as M V V S T M L N. Before we move on, I want to clarify how we focus on what is most important at each step. See figure 20.

Figure 20

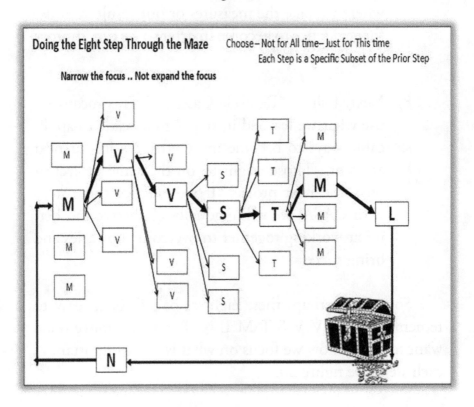

We want to simplify and concentrate our focus, improving our chances of success. Figure 20 shows how at each step, we create just one statement. There are many other possible statements to consider. We have to have the discipline to create and commit to just one. If everyone has a different idea for the mission or the strategy, chaos ensues.

For example, shown here are three alternative missions that could have been, but clearly were not chosen. We have to create just one, the right one for all of us and this situation. If we can't get our collective energies focused on just one, no plan that follows will ever work as we will each be working on different missions.

Each step narrows the focus for all that follow. We have to choose just one (1) Mission that best answers the question "For this specific challenge, what do we need to accomplish or master to meet our objective?" Once we have a mission defined, we need to create a (2) Vision only for that one specific mission. What would success look like for just that specific mission? There could be many visions, but we need to create just one that is shared and embraced by those involved at the exclusion of any other vision.

Once we have created a shared vision, we have to set (3) Values only for this specific vision, describing how we will proceed. There are many values to consider, but we need to select those most critical to just this effort. Then we need a (4) Strategy to fulfill this specific string of mission, vision, and values statements. This is doing the first four steps of the eight-step boogie in order, yet one step at a time. The strategy will be the launching pad for progress. Note how each step narrows the focus and thus improves our chances of success.

Once we have a strategy, we need to develop specific (5) Tactics to act on just this specific strategy. The strategy may have more than one but not too many listed efforts. There could be many tactics to consider, but we need to stay focused on just those needed for the major element of this specific strategy. These are specific tasks we will do. If it is not listed in the list of tactics, then we do not plan to do them as part of this strategy. Usually deciding what you won't do is challenging and liberating.

If the strategy has to have a lot of separate tactics, perhaps we have not defined our mission, vision, and values narrowly enough. Better to stop now and get this ironed out. A huge complex mission has many opportunities for failure. A narrower mission has more chance to succeed. We want to break the work down into bite-sized chunks where we can expect to be successful.

Big enough to make a difference,
small enough so we can
routinely be successful.

Once we have a tactics plan, we need to settle on ways to (6) Measure if we are actually performing the specific tactics. Then we use measures to see what we (7) Learned. And then we decide what we can do (8) Next. Next might be to return to our mission and refine it for the same project at a higher level of performance, or celebrate its achievement and move on to the next new challenge.

M V V S T M L N
So Easy…So Simple

At first, the eight steps seem overly complicated, like learning to ride a bicycle, and yet once we get familiar with it, we can do it without even thinking about it. Each step will eventually just come naturally to us. And in each subsequent action, we will just naturally do what is needed next. The first few trips through the eight steps are quite an experience of discovery and learning. Each time, it feels more natural.

> *Learning is being changed*
> *by the experience.*
> *—Unknown*

Finally, in order to overcome most any challenge, you have to do nearly the same set of steps anyway. However, most of us do them without any real known pattern of conscious thinking or plan about them. We just do what we have learned to do along the way. It just feels right to us. And unfortunately, few are naturally inclined to so clearly name the steps or measure the results: the big key to (1) learning, (2) being accountable, and (3) high performance.

The more this system is used to standardize the approach to the work, the more and more effective the staff will be at using the eight steps to stretch toward our high-level goals. Think CASA. When smart people across our organization understand the approach, it will be much easier than before when every person used different jargon, and each project or challenge was approached in a different way using different terms.

Think of the metrics, interpretation, outcome reviews, common working vocabulary, data sharing, filing processes, and collaboration that would be possible when the game plan for most every project was the same eight steps, relying on the same lexicon, while the content was tailored to each unique situation. This can be used for small projects and large projects that are broken into more manageable subprojects.

147

Now the focus can be on the content since the process approach is standardized, well-known, and in use by everyone! Learning, accountability, and performance all increase when the process is simple and clearly understood. Compare that to what you are likely doing now, where every challenge or project gets approached in a different way, with each person placed in charge doing what feels right to them, and none of these approaches match.

Also, people depart organizations, leaving records of their work with little explanation of the process they used. What if everyone in your organization normally used the same eight-step approach and terminology for projects? Would that make it easier to look back at past results with confidence?

Here again is my sports-related analogy that may be helpful to review it again to more fully understand and embrace its wisdom.

1. **Mission** = the specific game we are playing this time, not some other game or many games. Just this one specific game—be specific.
2. **Vision** = the inspiring image of future victory. State what success will look like exactly in three to five or appropriate time periods (weeks, months, years). This is stated as a specific date and as past tense.
3. **Values** = our best intentions and the rules we will play by for this specific game.
4. **Strategy** = our high-level game plan; key short high-level list only. If these won't do it, you don't have an effective strategy.

5. **Tactics** = our specific roles and actions as individuals. There are usually multiple tactics within each strategy item, but there should only be one process owner for each tactic.

6. **Measure** = the tally of our individual actions for each tactic and the total score. It's best to have both leading and lagging measures at each level.

7. **Learning** = comes from post-play, quarter, and game reviews of plays, metrics, and final outcomes. What did we learn to use in our next game?

8. **Next** = our newfound higher team performance capacity from having followed the steps with discipline and carefully considered what among our individual and collective learnings and actions are we now able to apply to our next challenge. Let's be sure our learnings are incorporated in our next plan. We are now more capable to play the next game, whatever it is.

Chapter Summary

This chapter expanded the basic four-step **PDCA** foundation for individuals and groups to the eight-step template. Built on the fundamental learning cycle, the eight-step template provides a reliable and effective road map for learning, accountability, and performance.

Now, in the next few chapters, let's move on to walk through each step with more precision.

CHAPTER 6

— ❧ —

PLAN: 1) Mission, 2) Vision, 3) Values, 4) Strategy

Chapter Summary

This chapter expands on P, the first step of **PDCA**, into the first four steps of the eight-step template. PLAN comes first for the simple reason it is the most important. Without a PLAN, everything that follows is chaos.

Before we begin the PLAN phase in detail, I want to share a way of thinking about this step that helps bring focus to our dialogues leading to higher-quality PLAN statements. We will be using this going forward. Please take a moment to study figure 21. This is a way of asking seven easy yet defining questions to bring clarity to our dialogue and statements. I call these the Seven Wise Wizards or just the Wizards.

Figure 21

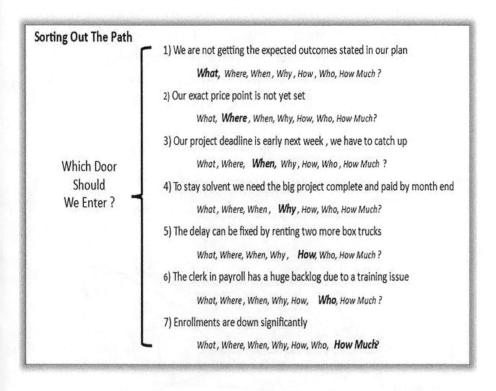

Sorting Out The Path

Which Door
Should
We Enter?

1) We are not getting the expected outcomes stated in our plan

What, Where, When, Why, How, Who, How Much?

2) Our exact price point is not yet set

What, **Where**, When, Why, How, Who, How Much?

3) Our project deadline is early next week, we have to catch up

What, Where, **When**, Why, How, Who, How Much?

4) To stay solvent we need the big project complete and paid by month end

What, Where, When, **Why**, How, Who, How Much?

5) The delay can be fixed by renting two more box trucks

What, Where, When, Why, **How**, Who, How Much?

6) The clerk in payroll has a huge backlog due to a training issue

What, Where, When, Why, How, **Who**, How Much?

7) Enrollments are down significantly

What, Where, When, Why, How, Who, **How Much?**

Each time we answer one of the Wizard's questions, we narrow the range of possibilities to consider further, making it easier to answer the next question. For example, let's say there is a broad range of opinions about the WHO of a project. Quality dialogue should lead to a consensus.

As we work our way through this process, we will likely discover that one or more of the Wizards can't be answered yet. This is helpful as it gets those that can be agreed upon out of the way, and it points to where we need to dig deeper to fully understand our challenge.

This improves our focus. We will be using the Wizards as we move through the rest of this process. See figure 22.

The cloud shape is our initial shared range of individual conceptions of the issue. The Wizards help us narrow our collective view in order to improve clarity, focus of action, and success. Quality, open, forward-looking dialogue initiated by sensitive leaders helps the group narrow focus. We are seeking alignment so all can support our final plan.

Figure 22

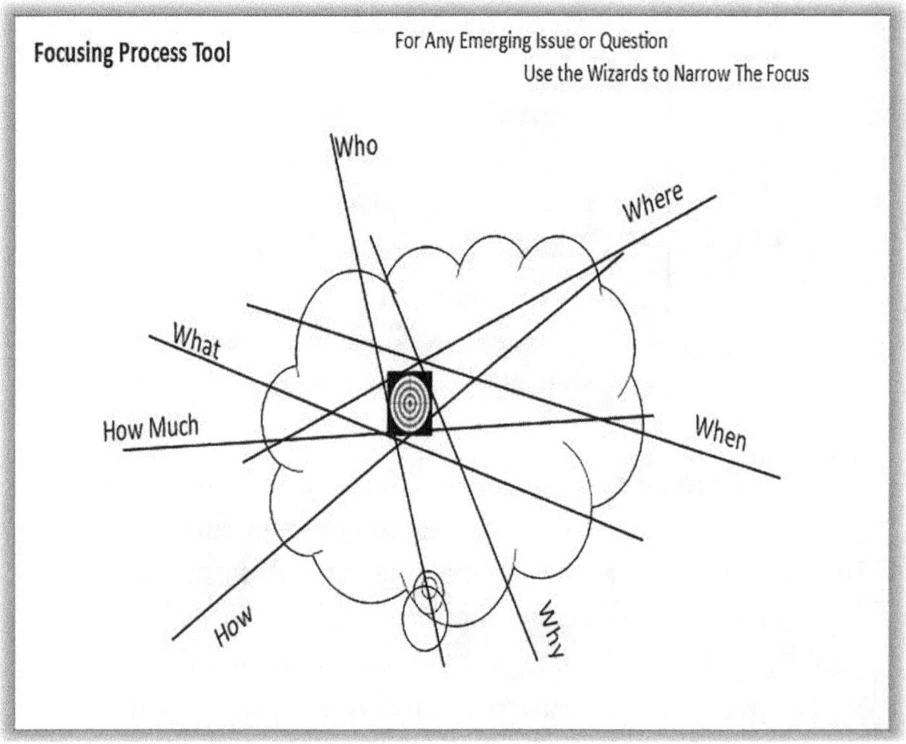

Focusing Process Tool

For Any Emerging Issue or Question
Use the Wizards to Narrow The Focus

Who

Where

What

How Much

When

How

Why

Each new consensus answer to one of the questions bisects the cloud as one of the Wizards is now satisfied. Continue on this path till all the Wizards are agreed upon, and you have narrowed the range of opinions to a very useful and powerful consensus for moving forward. This will be critical for effective shared action.

This shows how the amorphous cloud of possible choices can be narrowed by each of the Wizards. If we don't have the discipline to write down clear, crisp statements defining what we are going to DO, how can we ever expect to bring about the future we seek?

The use of the Wizards seems so easy, yet most of us are so focused on getting moving that we fail to take time to fully investigate the issue at hand to be sure we don't miss anything. Not every Wizard is needed every time, but better to ask them all every time in a CASA-disciplined way. If it is easy to come to consensus, you won't have wasted much time and you have established more firm ground for the group to work from.

Take a look at figure 23. Yes, it is a repeat of figure 21. It will be helpful to remember you can enter the problem space though any doorway, but in the end, you need to better understand all the ways to define and understand the key factors needed to solve the riddle. I encourage you to use the Wizards every time you define an issue. Think of each of the Wizards as just one doorway to better understand the issue.

Some will want to rush into problem-solving mode before opening every door. Be the leader who sets the pace by better defining the issue before setting off on the solution journey.

As a trial of this, go back in your mind and see how the Wizards can be used to define some work you are currently doing. Do all the key stakeholders agree on how you would answer the Wizards? Will the collective energies of your team be fully engaged if some think the answers are different? What effect will that have on your collective output?

Figure 23

Sorting Out The Path	
	1) We are not getting the expected outcomes stated in our plan
	What, *Where*, *When*, *Why*, *How*, *Who*, *How Much* ?
	2) Our exact price point is not yet set
	What, **Where**, *When*, *Why*, *How*, *Who*, *How Much?*
	3) Our project deadline is early next week , we have to catch up
Which Door	*What*, *Where*, **When**, *Why*, *How*, *Who*, *How Much* ?
Should	
We Enter ?	4) To stay solvent we need the big project complete and paid by month end
	What, *Where*, *When*, **Why**, *How*, *Who*, *How Much?*
	5) The delay can be fixed by renting two more box trucks
	What, *Where*, *When*, *Why*, **How**, *Who*, *How Much* ?
	6) The clerk in payroll has a huge backlog due to a training issue
	What, *Where*, *When*, *Why*, *How*, **Who**, *How Much* ?
	7) Enrollments are down significantly
	What, *Where*, *When*, *Why*, *How*, *Who*, **How Much?**

Now, back to the four PLAN steps. There has been so much written about them in the past five decades, I suspect you already have familiarity with them. I will just move forward laying out my take on them. You can find hundreds, if not thousands, of great articles and books about them.

I urge you to build a mental model for yourself for each as they will be valuable in anything you do. Here is my interpretation of them. What is different here is that they are all connected in a systems thinking–based template for success.

This is another place where the text may seem redundant. We have been over much of this before. This pass is intended to cement these ideas and fill any gaps in understanding to this point.

Finally, be careful about your final selection of words or phrases to describe each of the steps. Once you have a draft, work it over to be sure it does not contain any fuzzy wording that could be interpreted more than one way. For example, in a vision statement, we may be tempted to say "increase output significantly." What does that mean, exactly? Name the increase with a number and a time so that anyone can check to see if that vision was obtained. Best to make such a check with each statement once you have the basic idea down.

1) Mission Statement

Merriam-Webster: Mission.
"a specific task with which a person or a group is sent to perform"

The mission of a specific project you are doing, some corporate change plan, or a military effort, for example, may be to bring about a certain desirable result or avoid some less desirable future. The mission of an organization may be that it serves a specific role or purpose or seeks a valuable outcome. The mission of an individual may be to bring them fulfillment, peace, or perhaps wealth. The mission of a project may be that it solves some problem or brings harmony, profit, learning, innovation, or perhaps higher capacity.

Mission statements seem superfluous to people who unfortunately do not understand their value. Mission statements are critical to stating and understanding clearly what this particular activity is all about and, by difference, what it is not about. It is hard to solve a problem or gain some advantage you haven't yet fully defined. The mission statement defines the issue in very broad terms. The clearer and more focused the mission statement, the greater the chances of success in fulfilling the mission.

Mission statements need to be short and clear and supported by the next steps of vision, values, and strategy. They do not need to be so verbose they can stand on their own. The mission, vision, values, and strategy all have to fit together. And when they fit well, each can be quite short and direct since together, they make a whole. We don't want to expend our resources of time, talent, funds, etc., till we know exactly what we are going to DO and what outcome we seek.

There are all types of mission statements. Sometimes they are for a whole organization. Sometimes they are for an individual, and sometimes they are for a specific project. For the sake of our work here, let's say the mission statement needs to be for some specific project.

The most important aspect of the completed mission statement is that it remains front and center as the effort of those involved moves forward. They need to continually check to see that all subsequent investment of effort or resources are consistent and in service of this specific mission, nothing more, nothing less. Otherwise, we are wandering and not focused on the objectives of the mission.

> *If you don't know where you are going,*
> *any road will take you there.*
> *—Lewis Carroll*

> *(We have no clear destination,*
> *but we are working hard to get there!)*

Creating the PLAN statements is an iterative process. It will be necessary to first draft a (1) Mission statement for this specific project, then a (2) Vision statement in support of this specific mission, then a (3) Values statement in support of this specific mission and vision, then finally, a (4) Strategy statement that will outline generally how we will make it all happen. This is the "So What?" question. So what are you going to DO to make it happen? The mission, vision, values, and strategy are different for each project, tailored to the circumstances.

The set of PLANning statements serves a specific purpose in defining what this project is about, where we want to be when it is completed, how we will focus and behave on our journey, and the high-level approach we plan to take.

As each of these statements is drafted, you will need to go back and ensure that they are consistent with and in support of one another. It usually takes a few iterations to see that they are not in competition or conflict and, in fact, will all work together to make the project a success if the subsequent DCA steps are well taken. They do not have to be sentences, just key words that say explicitly what they are. The fewer distractions the better. If well-constructed, each of the four serves to clarify the others.

The mission says what the project is going to do. And by difference or absence, it also says what the project is not going to do. This is very important. Every project needs to have boundaries. Projects need clear, precise definition. Missions need to be specific in what they will do so no one is expecting them to do something else. The vision, values, and strategy need to support just this specific mission, not any other mission. If you need to also work on something else, then expand this mission statement, or better, create a separate stand-alone project to meet that need.

Example vague starting draft mission statements might be the following:

- Shave $40,000 off the energy budget at the Dallas plant
- Build an office building in San Antonio
- Get my MBA in finance
- Restore two acres of native grasses in the watershed
- Refine our time-reporting system

Each of these would have to be considered and rewritten to make them more actionable. Let's pick one and carry it forward as a working example. Let's say we chose "refine our time-reporting system" and use that as our example of a group effort. Remember the example from the sports analogy: **Mission** = the specific game we are playing this time, not some other game or many games. Just this one specific game. Be specific.

Our DRAFT working mission statement might be

1) *Mission: Within five months, refine our field labor hours reporting system in order to save money and become nimbler in estimating.*

This begins to define the **when, what,** and the **why** for the 7 Wizards.

Most will recognize the acronym "SMARTS" when setting goals. I have included that here in figure 24 if you are not familiar with it. We will revisit and use this frame multiple times.

Figure 24

The SMARTS Test

S specific   What exactly will you do?

M measurable   – As evidenced by ?

A achievable   – Resources and capacity available?

R relevant to our goals   – Important for our strategy ?

T timed   - Clear by when ?

S stretch   - Beyond our normal routine work ?

Read the draft mission example I provided imme-diately above and ask yourself if you think it could pass the SMARTS test if you knew the particulars about the situation.

Now go to the prior section, look over the vague start-ing draft missions I provided, and ask yourself if you think any of those mission statements could pass the SMARTS test?

2) Vision Statement

Merriam-Webster: Vision
"The act or power of anticipating that which will or may come to be"

The vision statement for the now-created draft specific mission is to make clear what future conditions will emerge if we are successful in implementing this specific mission.

> *Being happy doesn't mean everything's*
> *perfect, it means you've decided to*
> *see beyond the imperfections.*
> *—Albert Einstein*

The vision will describe what benefits will accrue, what outcomes will emerge, and what our system will be like if we are successful. It narrows and improves our level of understanding of the mission and the work ahead. It describes in vivid terms what inspires us to want to avidly pursue this mission because of the advantages it offers.

By its wording, the vision will be a positive statement about the future that inspires us to work hard toward its fulfillment. I like to say it makes the prize clear. It needs to be stated in past tense as if it had already happened.

> *The future is not some place we are going, but one we are creating. The paths are not to be found but made. And the activity of making them changes both the maker and the destination.*
> *—John Schaar*

Our DRAFT working vision statement might be

2) *Vision: Within 5 months, field reporting errors and rework have been reduced by 20%, payroll staff (of 9) reduced by one headcount, with that person moved over to support estimating, plus $50,000 per year saved by the inefficiencies reduced.*

Remember the example from our sports analogy: **Vision** = the inspiring image of future victory. State what success will look like exactly in some appropriate 3-to-5 period. Do you think this statement could pass the SMARTS test?

This adds more clarity for the **what, where, when, why, how, who, and how much** for those curious Wizards. Notice that the vision statement is given in past tense, as if it has already been accomplished. We are setting a course to attain a goal, not just working toward the goal. Not "I am working on it" but rather "I am on schedule on the

PLAN" or "We are behind schedule but are correcting and will complete on time."

3) Values Statement

Merriam-Webster: Values
"The abstract concepts of what is right, worthwhile, or desirable; principles or standards"

The values statement for a specific vision is to state the key needs of the project and the principles of conduct expected when working on this project. It sets parameters for behaviors as we pursue this specific mission and vision. It also names the practical critical factor considerations (like cost, transparency, time, respect, accuracy, inclusiveness, or efficiency) we will pay most attention to.

By its wording, our values statement also guides our interactions and the standards of fairness we will observe. By its wording, it will be a positive inspiration that compels us to act within agreed-upon parameters with fairness and honesty.

> *The competition is out*
> *there, not in here.*
> *Let's behave like we know that.*

Our DRAFT working values statement might be
3) *Values: This team will involve those most affected, improve accuracy, focus on fact-driven, cost-reducing improvements, learn how to best proceed, make, vet,*

and implement a timely plan with key stakeholders,
and implement the plan on time.

This brings even more clarity for the **who, what, when,** and **how** to satisfy those pesky Wizards. Do you think this statement passes the SMARTS test?

I think of values on two levels. There are the more practical hard values for any project, like timeliness, accuracy, cost control, etc., and the more authentic leadership values like sensitivity, tact, perception, and inclusion. Notice I did not say dominance or control. Think of them like guidelines. We all hold different opinions of what timeliness, accuracy, and all the rest actually mean.

To some, practical values and authentic leadership values are just general notions of how things need to be, and to others, these are strict clear definitions. If a team commits to any one of these for a project, it would be most helpful if they spent some time actually chatting about what such a behavior and outcome would look like. This will forestall stress later when individual working differences show up in their interactions.

There can be a tendency among weak leaders and groups to think of values like slogans or logos, simple signs or banners to put up to show you at least talked about them. Project failures can usually be tracked back to a lack of clarity and commitment to shared intentions. This is where the wheels come off the wagon. The failure is explained as lack of resources or something else when deeply shared values and commitment could have easily overcome the obstacle.

As for the more authentic (very hard) leadership values, I tend to think of them not so much as a value you want or have or need on this project, but rather that the value actually has you! Think about that a bit. You act out of your natural values. You don't have values; your values have you! We act out of our natural mental states. If sensitivity is part of our makeup, then that will just naturally be present in our behaviors. If we don't have that, it will be hard to get. Stating these very hard values leading to an in-depth dialogue about how they are needed in some project will put all on notice.

In any team or group, each person will be somewhere on the continuum of any one value, from barely understanding it to deeply committed to it. When the wheels wobble off the wagon, the team dialogue will eventually reveal which value was violated or ignored.

The values need to be agreed upon in advance and posted and periodically revisited. This way these quiet, behind-the-scenes yet powerful guidelines can be used to keep the behaviors of the team on track.

Remember the example from our sports analogy: **Values** = our best intentions and the rules we will play by for this specific game.

4) Strategy Statement

Merriam-Webster: Strategy
"A plan or method for achieving a specific goal"

The strategy statement for a specific mission is to state our general high-level approach to address the intention of this specific mission. We certainly will have a number of simultaneous missions for different challenges. This statement is the strategy for just this one effort or challenge. It is not detailed down to action steps; that will come in tactics.

The value of a strategy statement is to test with stakeholders if this approach is deemed likely to succeed. Does it contain all the right major elements to meet the challenge of this mission? Is it a clear high-level plan that will elicit commitment on the part of those needed for its implementation?

If the strategy statement fails on the last two factors, it is doomed. This statement is not intended to be a list of specific tasks. On the other hand, I think it can at a high level be SMARTS—that is specific, measurable, achievable, relevant, timed, and a stretch.

> *People argue less about the ends*
> *but routinely argue about the*
> *means. Get the means narrowed*
> *to a good PLAN now before it is*
> *too late and we have already*
> *started wasting resources.*

When you go back and read the mission, vision, values, and then this strategy, are they consistent? Do they support and enhance each other? Do they convince you this is the way to proceed? This is a key testing point. Notice that since they are all about the same project, none of them have to be wordy. One needs to read all four to capture the essence of this PLAN.

If any of the key stakeholders have serious qualms about the adequacy of the mission, vision, values, or strategy statements, stop and re-cycle now to bring agreement before you start expending resources on a failed PLAN. You do not want to start on a PLAN that is not fully supported, or you will be back at the beginning again soon, starting over.

***The easy way out usually leads
to doing it over again.***

Our DRAFT working strategy statement might be:
4) *Strategy: Within five months, we will:*

    a) *Assign responsibility to a cross-functional team, including field managers and payroll staff*
    b) *Study the process and past three years of error rework to identify best opportunities*
    c) *Build and implement a metrics dashboard system to track errors and improvements*
    d) *Provide dashboard feedback to each field manager every pay period*
    e) *Build and teach a time reporting training class for all field managers*
    f) *Post and coach metrics outcomes at each monthly field Mgrs. Meeting*
    g) *Reduce payroll staff by moving one person to the estimating function cost center, once 20 percent error reduction goal reached and savings rate captured*

This provides a high-level seven-step action list for the **what, where, when, why, how, who, and how much** for those lousy little Wizards. Please note there is little detail telling specifically **how** each of these will be done. Strategy statements show the very high level **how.** Full detail will come in the next step with our tactic's statements.

Remember the example from our sports analogy: **Strategy**: our high-level game plan, key short high-level list only. If these won't do it, you don't have an effective strategy.

A way to test for an effective strategy statement is to ask yourself if you could tell a stranger or your aging aunt Millie what your plan was in less than two minutes, and they would understand and accept it as logical and complete. How much detail would you want to provide? When those called upon to work on the plan learn of it, they need to see a simple list of overall high-level strategy actions that make sense and fit together in a logical fashion within the logical set of likely resource constraints.

Those called upon for implementation need to see that their part of it will fit with the others and make it a success. If they don't, you need to go back and re-cycle. We are trying to bite off just enough of a challenge that we succeed, yet just a bit less challenge than would allow us to fail. I call this a stretch. We want to be an organization that moves ever forward on a steady diet of success by stretching ourselves. This is (a) learning, (b) being accountable, and (c) continuing high performance.

People do not want to be held accountable for challenges beyond their control or capacity. They do want to be held accountable for challenges they can master and demonstrate competency. So the capacity of the team is part of the equation. The role of the leader is to assimilate all these pieces to be sure the team and effort are moving steadily forward on a diet of consistent and systematic successes. CASA again. Also, the leader needs to ensure the people tasked with this challenge have the understanding, resources, and authority they need to make it work.

The way we each and together behave as we proceed (the project values exhibited in our behaviors) will have a lot to do with whether we are successful. The shared level of commitment to a strategy is worth much more than the actual technical quality of the strategy.

Most strategy efforts fail due to lack of commitment, not lack of an effective strategy, clear tactics, or even resources. There has been much written about this in the past several decades. Lack of commitment comes from lack of clear direction, skill, or time and resources.

Culture eats strategy for breakfast.
—Peter Drucker

If the culture as exhibited in the Values statement supports openness and shared learning, then collaborative edits to the draft PLAN statements will build support and cohesion for moving forward. If the words in the values statement are just fancy, meaningless, nice-sounding words, the outcome will be compromised. The worst values statement is the one that everyone hails and salutes and then ignores. Do we really have a SHARED PLAN, or do we have a PLAN SHARED?

Chapter Summary

This chapter expanded on P, the first step of **PDCA**, into the first four steps of the eight-step template. PLAN comes first for the simple reason it is the most important. Without a PLAN, everything that follows is chaos.

Good PLANs resonate with us as aspirational. They clarify our destination, they give us inspiration, and they open the door to exploration of what more is possible for us.

Now let's move on to how to actually make the PLAN come alive.

CHAPTER 7

— ∽ —

DO: 5) Tactics

Chapter Summary

This chapter expands on DO, the second step of **PDCA**, by exploring how to use Tactics to get things done. A huge part of quality detailed planning is ensuring there will be adequate resources to actually complete our emerging plan. We will explore tactics in the face of realistic assessment of capacity. Additionally, we will select one tactic and lay out how to proceed, laying the groundwork for the actual metric for it, which will be covered in chapter 9.

Tactics Statements

Merriam-Webster: Tactic
"A plan, procedure, or expedient for promoting a desired end"

The tactics needed for a specific strategy are a list of the very detailed actions needed to fulfill the elements of the strategy. They are the DOing in the PLAN. Most of us really like the DOing part of plans. It is where we can demonstrate our skill. It is usually where we get the most acknowledgment and sense of fulfillment. No wonder so many of us are stuck on DO at the expense of the rest of P, C, and A. To many, the DOing feels like fun, and the P, C, and A steps feel like work.

There can and will likely be multiple tactics for each statement in the strategy. Taken all together, they should make clear exactly how the project will proceed. If the strategy is robust enough and tactics are completed, the mission and vision should be fulfilled. This is typically where project management skills kick in. Tactics lists can't be told in an elevator speech. Tactics need to be written down and measurable most of the time. We will address the measuring part in the next chapter.

This chapter is short since this is an area most of us are already proficient. Making lists of actions to be taken is a natural path for most of us. That said, there is a tendency to even skimp on this step since we are so familiar with it. We may unwittingly create our own poor performance by leaving out small but important steps that protect us from process failures.

Think of the 1986 space shuttle disaster where lack of focus on details killed seven astronauts. This is where discipline can save us from ourselves. High performers have discipline, the discipline of detail and completion (think airline pilot discipline!).

Got the Needed Resources?

But first, let's talk about resources. In the steps till now, we have not spoken of the issue of having adequate resources. The mission, vision, values, and strategy were about creating an inspiring high-level plan. Once we have a strategy, we embark on detailed steps to make that happen: tactics. This is where we think about what it will actually take to make the vision come true. We can't really assess resource needs till we know for certain exactly what we are trying to do.

The steps of the tactics will reveal exactly what resources will be needed. We need to know if we have enough of the following:

1. Time
   a) Before time runs out and we crash
   b) Before the opportunity is closed to us
   c) Within current working capacity: in days, hours
   d) Etc.
2. People
   a) To staff this work while also doing current work
   b) Access to contract forces to assist
   c) Etc.
3. Talent
   a) Do we currently have or can timely acquire the skills needed?
   b) Patience and sensitivity
   c) Etc.

4. Space
    a) Office, warehouse, plant
    b) Store shelf space
    c) Etc.
5. Equipment
    a) Trucks, machines, computers
    b) Etc.
6. Materials
    a) Raw materials in adequate supply chain
    b) Utilities
    c) Computing time
    d) Etc.
7. Desire
    a) Collective commitment to take this on now
    b) Etc.
8. Funding
    a) Budget, budget authority
    b) Working cash
    c) Etc.

For each line item in each tactic step, the needed resources need to be assessed. Does our system have the capacity to add in yet another task? Above are just a few aspects of the resources needed. You will need to tailor your plans to be realistic about them in your world. You will likely need other categories. If/when you find they are insufficient, you have learned!

At least you learned this well before you are halfway into a new plan that will fail due to lack of resources. Most of us just worry about the funding as if that is all there is to worry about, and then later fail when the other resources are not available.

We may have most of what we need. But we may be short some critical element that will block progress on the entire project. We need to be smart enough to know the law of the minimum applies to us.

The law of the minimum, also called Liebig's law of the minimum, is a law about the growth of plants. It states that the growth of a plant is limited by the resource that is most scarce, and not by the total amount of resources available. The law has also been used to predict the growth of populations.

Assessing resources as matched against the mission, vision, values, and strategy is a key step. In fact, I would say this is where most plans fail. Each new project brings untold demands on current capacity. Wise leaders know best to not start something you can't successfully finish. So before we ever start a new project, we ensure the resources are available and that adding this new project won't throw all our other ongoing work to the trash heap by drawing critical scarce resources to some new project at the expense of ongoing work. This means assessing not just resources for this project, but how this new work fits in all the other ongoing work.

Realistic assessment of resource constraints rule PLAN success!

Talented authentic leaders do the hard work of balancing all the demands for work currently underway and now being added. Just adding more work to the pile is a fool's errand.

Now, back to tactics. I think doing projects is a lot like doing a good job of tying your shoelaces. If you do a good job, you won't notice them, have to mess with them, or trip over them. If you do a sloppy job of tying your shoes, they will put you in harm's way of tripping over them all day. If you have to stop and retie them, you will have spent more time than it would have taken to do it right in the first place. The easy way out usually leads back in!

> *If you want to change the world,*
> *start off by making your bed.*
> *—Admiral William McRaven told*
> *the graduating class of 2014 at*
> *the University of Texas, Austin*

> **What the navy counts as "making*
> *your bed" (square corners, centered*
> *pillow, blanket neatly folded at the*
> *foot of the rack) is idiosyncratic.*
> *Yet the admiral's broader point is*
> *universal: whether you are a sailor,*
> *a salesperson, or CEO, "if you make*
> *your bed every morning, you will have*
> *accomplished the first task of the day."*
> *His commencement speech went viral.*

> **Discipline drives details that matter.**
> **—*Economist Business*, "Your**
> **Inner Dawdler," 9/17/22**

Tactics are the essence of the PLAN. As such, they need to be written down clearly and completely. Our DRAFT working tactics statements will be much more complicated than the statements up till now. They will be lists of clear specific tasks, at least one for each item of this strategy, perhaps more. The tactics need to specify who will do what by when exactly. We get to use those Wizards again!

Additionally, some tasks will have to be measurable and measured. After the tactics statements are drafted, the measures will be developed. If the specific tasks are not readily measurable, we will need to cycle back and edit the tactics task lists so they effectively support the strategy and are also measurable. If we can't measure it, then we developed the wrong tactic, or we have not been creative enough in our approach to measurement.

> ***If you can't measure it,***
> ***you can't manage it.***
> ***—W. Edwards Deming***

For our working example, we will take just the first three strategy actions and draft some example tactics statements for them. A real project will certainly read differently. See the following tables for examples of tactics.

4) Strategy – Within the next five months, we will

   a) *Assign responsibility to a cross-functional team, including field managers and payroll staff*
   b) *Study the process and past three years of error rework to identify best opportunities*
   c) *Build and implement a metrics dashboard to track errors and improvements,*

Figures 25, 26, and 27 show what these look like in detail.

It takes discipline and clear thinking to build the tactics charts needed to ensure we are being true to our M, V, V, and S. Notice there are spaces in the tables to insert tasks. These are just rough drafts, ready for edit by a team. Perhaps the team will add steps or make edits to make the tactics more direct and actionable. I have laid out a fairly simple hypothetical set of tasks for the first three-line items in this example strategy.

Figure 25 First Set of Tactics for Strategy Statement 4

4 a) Assign responsibility to a cross functional team , include field managers and payroll staff

Tactic	Step	Tasks to be completed on time within the larger schedule	Process Owner
4 a	1	Assign a team leader as process leader for entire strategy	Manager
	2	Set a master schedule for each task to be completed within five months	Team Lead
	3	Form a cross functional team; 3 field managers , and 3 payroll staff	Team Lead, W/ Mgr. Support
	4	Set / share monthly progress against plan milestones and check points	Team Lead

Figure 26. Second Set of Tactics for Strategy Statement 4

4 b) Study the process and past 3 years of error rework to identify best opportunities

Tactic	Step	Tasks to be completed on time within the larger schedule	Process Owner
4 b	1	Identify field and office processes to be improved by gathering and studying error rates by type for past three years	Team Lead
	2	Select highest frequency error types to improve efficiency by 20%	Team
	3	Make improvements to processes to reduce errors	Team
	4	Estimate rework time savings in payroll and field offices	Team

Figure 27 Third Set of Tactics for Strategy Statement 4

4 c) Build and implement a metrics dashboard system to track errors and improvements

Tactic	Step	Tasks to be completed on time within the larger schedule	Process Owner
4 c	1	Set schedule for creating metrics dashboards for field managers	Team Lead
	2	Set schedule for creating the process to share results	Team Lead
	3	Create systematic metrics dashboard for each field manager	Team
	4	Implement plan for sharing results	Team
	5	Ensure this phase completed on schedule within 5 months	Team Lead

Notice I show the name of the process leader for each step. In some cases, that would a team. In other cases, that would be a specific name. We need to build accountability into our work and make only one person accountable for each task if we can. At this stage, it is time to build in the accountability we want for our project and our culture. Enter names! If you can't enter a specific name, then make the supervisor of that group the person responsible for that tactic. We want to know Who Will Do What By When

W W D W B W
See, accountability is so easy!

If this were your real project, the wording would be different, and perhaps there would be more or fewer tasks. These are just examples of the kind of tasks needed. A PLAN will never be fully viable if you can't lay out the specific strategy, tactics, process owners, and measures in advance. Without these, you don't really have a PLAN; you have an intention to work toward something, but not a PLAN.

Once you have a working draft list of tactics, you will want to test them against those old Wizards to ensure we have covered the bases. This step adds even more clarity for the what, where, when, why, how, who, and how much for the curious Wizards.

Here is an example test of the value of using the Wizards. Here is my assessment of step 4b to see if we are getting clear on what we need to be focused on during the DO phase. I think we have. If you can't agree, then go back and refine the statements till you do agree. Please take a look at figure 28.

Figure 28. What would the Wizards say?

For 4 b) Study the processes and past 3 years of error rework to identify best opportunities.

Wizard	Clarify
What	Identify processes to be improved
Where	Process manuals and error records by type, field and office
When	Study last 3 years , complete this study consistent with project schedule
Why	Identify specific opportunities to improve operations
How	Team reviews processes and records, design and implement improvements
Who	Team
How Much	Improve efficiency by 20%

It takes discipline to get good at this. Once you do, it will be easy to look at any set of tasks and make quality tactics plans. I suggest you work with others to create the tactics charts, then get all the actual participants and stakeholders to agree the tactics satisfy the Wizards and pass the SMARTS test.

Chapter Summary

This chapter expanded on D, the second step of **PDCA**, by exploring how to use Tactics to get things done. This chapter was more about formation of detailed plans and anticipation of actually doing the work. A key component of a good tactic is that there will be adequate resources to actually do it. If you can't say with certainty that you are all set with resources, stop and go back to revise your mission, vision, values, and strategy. Be the smart one who got all this right before you start down the road.

Now let's move on to the Measure step in chapter 8. There are actually two chapters on measure. The first one is a general overview of measures, and the second one works up examples of measures for the example project we have been discussing.

CHAPTER 8

———— ✑ ————

DO: 6) Measure—General Overview

Chapter Summary

This chapter expands more on DO, the second step of **PDCA**, by exploring how to use Measures to follow and ensure things get done as planned. You will notice I use the terms *measures* and *metrics* interchangeably. This chapter explores the basics of measurement that can be a complex subject in its own right. We will cover general ideas about building measures here and then, in the next chapter, work on specific examples from our case above.

Please note this chapter contains a number of different ways of looking carefully at something to be measured. As tools, I have included more than you would need or use regularly. My intent is to share multiple frameworks with the intent some of them will help you. Do not be put off by the apparent redundancy.

There are excellent sources of information for how to analyze things. The best single summary book I have ever found is *The Memory Jogger Plus* + by Michael Brassard. Even if you never pursue the ideas in the book in your hand, I urge you to get *The Memory Jogger Plus* + for your work.

The eight-step template comes alive when we can analyze the challenge before us, make and implement a plan, measure our work, be accountable, learn from it, and experience successful outcomes.

This chapter should make it easier for you to apply the value of the eight-step template more rapidly. It assumes you don't know much about metrics yet and want to learn more. For some it will be refresher. Some experienced readers may just choose to move to the next chapter.

Metrics is a huge topic. We can't adequately cover it as part of a short book on the eight-step template. I urge you to study about metrics independently to improve your range and depth of knowledge in this critical area.

> *I have been struck by how important measurement is to improving the human condition. You can achieve incredible progress if you set a clear goal and find a measure that will drive progress toward that goal. That may seem basic, but it is amazing how often it is not done and hard it is to get right.*
> —*Bill Gates*

The internet has a wealth of information, and here are a few books I have found helpful: *Counting What Counts* by Marc Epstein and Bill Birchard, *Keeping Score* by Mark

Graham Brown, and *Performance Measurement* by Jerry Harbor. Don't be put off by the fact they are from the past; other than technology applications, basic measurement has not changed in decades.

If, after reading a bit of this chapter, you find your mind wandering due to all the details, I urge you to jump ahead to the next chapter and come back to this when you need to get serious about measurement. Creating effective measures is not always easy. Later, after you've digested the whole eight-step process, if you are intrigued by this process and ready to give it a try, then you can come back here and the next chapter and go through the steps to create some measures.

Don't be put off by the complexity of metrics; focus on finding metrics that are valuable for your work, easy to build, and easy to use from among the many you will learn about if you pursue independent study. Figure 29 shows just a few of the many types of measures to use to better describe your process outcomes.

8) Measure Statements

Merriam-Webster: Measure
"The act or process of ascertaining the extent, dimensions, or quantity of something"

Figure 29

Measurement Types

      Quantity :
            Frequency [sales calls made]
            Rate [how often something happens or does not happen]
            Percent [performance occurs divided by number of attempts]

      Quality :
            Accuracy .. [number of errors]
            Novelty [ratings of behavior– creation of a new process]
            Appearance [compared to some objective standard]

    Resources / Cost:
            Labor [hours , set up time, delays, rework]
            Material [inventory , tools, waste , theft, vehicles, fuel]
            Mgmt. [time spent organizing and following work]

      Time :
            Duration [weeks in a project, delays]
            Timeliness [on time vs. delays]
            Latency [delay getting started once planned]
            Completion [finish]

We measure things to better understand them and to know if they have changed. We measure things in context with other things for relative change over time. Measurement is a critical path to (1) learning, (2) accountability, and (3) high performance, our key objectives.

> ***Measure for the primary purposes
> of learning and influencing,
> then maybe for controlling!***

If you don't really know what happened, how can you honestly recover, celebrate, learn, or adjust based on just guesses or opinion? **PDCA** is based on the premise that we know what we tried to do and we know with certainty what actually happened so we can adapt our PLAN and move ahead based on facts. Ahhhh, learning! Great friends, those facts!

> *How you gather, manage, and*
> *use information will determine*
> *whether you win or lose.*
> *—Bill Gates*

After some preliminary sharing of general ideas about metrics, I will provide processes and examples for two kinds of measures, (a) step by step progress and (b) and incremental change in one factor over time, in the form of Behavior Over Time charts (BOTs).

Before we go deeper, a word about technology. Computers are wonderful machines. They can make our work much easier when we harness their power correctly. However, I think we need to fully understand what we are measuring first. This can be like giving your elementary school–aged child a calculator too early, and then they never actually master the basics of simple math. The machine is no better than the person using it.

Once we understand the process well, metrics can be automated with computer systems. Fancy tables, charts, graphs, and data collection systems are cool. They are especially cool if they actually present important, factual, and measured data in useful ways. Learn the methods of metrics before you start to automate them.

> *A fool with a tool is still a fool.*
> *Power tools can accelerate failure!*

I urge you to start your metrics improvements with pencil and paper. Dance with the Wizards on paper first. Get the content right before you make it fancy. There may be tendency to skip over the deep thinking needed for effective measures in the rush to make a fancy graphic outcome.

We want to be sure we are measuring things that will truly make a difference and move us forward in understanding and outcome (learning, accountability, and performance), not just a fancy presentation that makes an impression and leads to nothing.

Once you have developed a metric, ask yourself, "So what? How will we use this information to make a difference? Is there another metric more worthy of our attention?" If this metric appears to be the big driver of performance, you are done. If there are other factors that may be bigger drivers of performance, put this one aside and work on the factor with more leverage. This can be hard to do. Be sure you are measuring the factors that most influence the outcome.

There are many ways to measure things. Unfortunately, most people think measures have to be complex to be meaningful, causing them to shy away from even trying to make good measures. I suggest you strive to build and rely on measures that are easy to construct, understand, and use to (1) learn, (2) promote accountability, and (3) drive performance. Don't be afraid to start with one measure and then upgrade it once you see it is not as important as you thought. That is **PDCA** in action. Ahhhh, learning!

Measurement can be complex, and it requires discipline. It is the key link in the chain of learning. Without good data, we are just operating with opinions and our fallible memories. In fact, I think it is one of the most critical elements in our pursuit of learning, accountability, and performance.

> *Without solid measures,*
> *it is impossible to build*
> *on prior experience.*
> *—Unknown*

More, I think the lack of familiarity with measurement is why many organizations are stuck; they have the resources they need but can't get them deployed effectively because they avoid the disciplined hard work of actually learning by measurement what actually works and what does not work. It is better to measure what matters with less-than-perfect accuracy than to measure something with high accuracy that does not matter much.

Remember the example from our sports analogy: Measures = the tally of our individual actions for each tactic and the total score. Imagine a sports team that did not keep tally of players actions and the score! It's best to have both leading and lagging measures at each level, which we will cover soon.

Begin with "What results do I need, and how can I measure that," rather than "what measures can I get?" What you measure should influence organizational behavior. If it doesn't, you need a better measure. What you don't measure has lower chance of occurring. Think carefully about what you are measuring and why. Measures should be few in number, drive important outcomes, be easily understood, and easily linked to desired results.

Figure 30 gives some examples of different types of metrics. In many organizations, facts are interesting, but opinions matter more. And unfortunately and frequently, the position and status of the opinion holder matters even more. However, to be learners, we need to move beyond that with evidence-based decision-making regardless of opinions. Memories and opinions vary over time and are no substitute for well-planned metrics and the facts they can bring to light for all to see.

I urge you to be the leader who sets the tone and culture for the organization to move to processes where measurement provides process results that are accepted as facts, and then those facts are used to drive decisions. Save your opinions for politics, religion, and sports for the weekend camping trip.

Even if you are not the so-called leader, you can make and use effective measures to improve your own performance area and thus differentiate yourself from most of the rest who will not make the effort.

Figure 30

Which Type of Measure is Best ?

RESULTS	PROCESS	VALUE CREATORS
LAG MEASURES	WORK IN PROGRESS	LEAD MEASURES
Production	Units Under Construction	Production Capacity
Outputs	Working inventory	Inputs
Reactive	Monitoring	Predictive
Financial	Accumulating Costs Yet Invoiced	Pre-Financial
Process	Work Hours Scheduled	People
Doing	Testing Approaches	Learning
Hard Measures	Accumulating Hard Data Yet Filed	Soft [very hard] Measures
Objective	Fact Based Guessing	Subjective
Internal	Interpreting External	External

Back of the bus ... Side of the bus ... Front of the bus

Many call this evidence-based leadership. I urge you to read more about this in the book *Hard Facts, Dangerous Half-Truths, and Total Nonsense* by Jeffrey Pfeffer and Robert I. Sutton. Let's start with which type of measure to use.

Study figure 30 again for a few minutes. Try to apply these ideas to just one aspect or your own organization's efforts.

Simple measures are about end-of-process results. Smarter measures are about the results plus the capacity and effort that bring about those results and what needs to be done now/next. I call these value creators. For example, we can and should measure production. But what if we also measured production capacity? This might be a much better measure of what the future could hold. Production tells us what we did, and production capacity tells us what we can do.

Certainly, we can and should measure outputs; in fact, those measures are the easiest of all. But we should also measure inputs being consumed as smarter, more holistic measures of our system.

Most results measures are like looking out the back of the bus; they only show where we have been. By time we see a trend out the back window, it may be too late to make timely effective corrections before the crash. Better measures look out the side windows, showing what is going on right now. These measure work in progress (WIP). WIP measures give us better information, yet still are late in the process. By now we have spent resources on supplies, made commitments, invested labor, etc. Usually at this point, it is too late in the process to make meaningful changes.

Work-in-Progress measures can be an effective early warning system.

It is much better to look out the front window and focus on what we are going to do next to ensure future results are headed in the right direction.

If we are good at actually doing what we say we are going to do, then leading measures may be the best. Measures of past performance are called lag measures. Measures of current performance are called WIP measures. Measures of value creators are called lead measures. We usually need all three.

Now that we have the basics, you may find the examples in figure 31 helpful to study. Some things are hard to quantify. We want to begin by asking what lead measure would be most helpful in fact-based decision-making about our future. We don't want to start with what is easiest to measure. Lag measures are the easiest and where most people focus when first developing a metrics plan.

That is fine as long as your system then evolves toward ever more and more effective meaningful measures closer to where actions can lead to success. Challenge yourself at this moment to assess what measures you currently use and whether they are lag, work-in-progress, or lead measures. Just doing that will bring you to a new level of awareness and perhaps improvement.

Lag measures are usually called hard measures since they are usually based on numbers that are already a product of our systems like expenses, profit, production outputs, etc. Work-in-progress measures like labor hours, invoices sent, etc., tell us if we are doing the right things at the right rate. They are frequently also available since there is a data stream as work-in-progress resources are being consumed.

Just be sure the work-in-progress measures focus on the human side of the system since that is where all the leverage is. Counting wheelbarrows on the job won't help. Counting how many man-hours were spent moving wheelbarrows on each job may.

Lead measures are usually called soft measures since they seem to measure the "soft" things like attitudes, customer reorder churn rate, sales calls, preproduction orders, etc. Lead measures are really the "very hard" measures since they are much harder to measure well, and they are usually much more meaningful for predicting future success even if less accurate. Lead measures are usually hard to create since they by necessity require more guessing, yet they can be the most effective predictor of future success.

Now take a long look at figure 31. See if you can figure out what metrics you have that are similar to these. See if you can envision making metrics in all three categories. See if you can sense which type of metric would be most likely to lead your organization to success.

Now considering the ideas in this chapter on measurement and at the risk of boring you again, I suggest you again use the SMARTS test. See figure 32. We used this a bit earlier in the text. You may have seen or used this is in the past. The trouble is many know about it, but few actually use it in its most useful form as it seems too simple. Imagine that! Yet another example of poor discipline that compromises success.

This should be applied after the first four PLAN statements (mission, vision, values, and strategy) are initially drafted. It will help test to see if the first four statements are likely to succeed. If your PLAN statements can't easily pass the SMARTS test, go back and edit them till they can.

Figure 31

Example Lag, Work In Progress, and Lead Measures

	Lag Measures = Past	Work In Progress= Now	Lead Measures = Future
Company Or Dept Examples	✓ Sales ✓ Safety improved ✓ EE* skill capacities ✓ Accident Rate reduced ✓ Total Sales	❖ Scheduled Sales calls ❖ Safety plans working ❖ New skills emerging ❖ Workforce training underway ❖ Bids in process	❑ Sales Prospects ❑ Safety awareness campaign ❑ Technical training scheduled ❑ Training budgeted/ scheduled ❑ Proposals out for consideration
	✓ Employee satisfaction / retention ✓ Customer Satisfaction ✓ Employee work output	❖ Leadership Behaviors ❖ Employees sensitive to customers needs ❖ Employee dedication / efforts	❑ Shared Values ❑ Shared Vision ❑ Shared Mission
Examples For Emerging Leaders	✓ Productive team	❖ Steadily improving output	❑ Team training
	✓ Lower accident rate	❖ Safe behaviors practiced	❑ Require safe behaviors
	✓ More knowledgeable	❖ Ideas digested/ things tried	❑ Study tolearn and grow
	✓ Get promoted	❖ Take on new challenges	❑ Get feedback, learn all I can
	✓ Get a raise	❖ More output each time	❑ Find better methods
	✓ Cooperative culture	❖ Sharing of resources	❑ Help others succeed too
	✓ Accountability culture	❖ Jobs on schedule	❑ Track & coach performance

Sometimes what counts can't be (easily) counted, and what can be counted (easily) doesn't count.
—Albert Einstein

Note that hope is not listed as one of the SMARTS elements! If the tactics statements can't pass the SMARTS test, now is the time to re-cycle and make sure they do. There is no sense going forward if you can already see the strategy is flawed. The tighter and more logical the strategy and tactics, the more those implementing them will want to work on them. No one wants to work on projects that appear incomplete, vague, flawed, or deemed to fail at the start.

Figure 32

Does My Intended Lead Effort , Work in Progress , or Lag Measure Pass the SMARTS Test?

S_pecific : Exactly what will be done ?

    An uninvolved observer would understand it exactly and who will do it?

M_easurable: As shown by what facts / evidence ?

    Expressed from this to that format ? Does the lead effort evidence track progress over time ?

A_chievable : Are resources available , obstacles manageable, and within control ?

    Within existing abilities with the resources available? Adequate opportunity of time and cooperation?

R_elevant: Is this the most important thing to be doing now?

    Is this in line with larger strategies both short and long term ?

T_imed : Specifically , in detail ?

    Are the milestones and end point clear in time ?

S_tretch: Challenges to achieve more than doing already ?

    Is this a good balance between being achievable and pushing to achieve more than before?

Bad news is usually suppressed and late in arriving. We want good news and bad news to surface at the same rate so changes can be made to limit damage and/or grasp opportunities. I call this no-surprise metrics. If the system is working well, important trends will become evident in the work-in-progress data about efforts as news steadily flows, good and bad, to decision-makers.

Good metrics would have us knowing things were going haywire before this shows up in the lag measures, or we are stuck in some process where we continue to waste resources because we do not yet know this is a failed process. We want to see graphics because when the data is presented in graphic form, trends are much more easily detected. Emerging trends can then be investigated using the five whys.

> **Those who cannot remember the past are condemned to repeat it.**
> **—George Santayana**

Back to the Five Whys

Repeating here from chapter 1, the Five Whys are a way of digging deeper to find the root cause of outcomes. Let's say your car won't start. This example from Wikipedia will help you find the root cause:

Why? – The battery is dead.
Why? – The alternator is not functioning.
Why? – The alternator belt has broken.

Why? – The belt was well beyond its useful service life and not replaced.

Why? – The vehicle was not maintained
according to the recommended service schedule.

The answer to the fifth Why is usually the root cause, the one to focus on. What do you want to work on, the initial manifestation of the root cause or the root cause itself?

I think the most successful organizations pursue a method of standardizing the way things are measured, reported, and acted upon. When every person or small group creates their own metrics in isolation, there is no opportunity to easily gather and digest them or "roll them up" into larger sets of key indicators that are the key drivers to success for the whole organization. Moreover, many do not ensure there is a central collection place of all metrics, further compromising the potential learning from looking at evidence from the past. You paid for them, why not collect and value them? Create a file that accumulates your operating history. Save every measure even if you are not sure how it will be useful in the future.

This is an argument for CASA in your metrics efforts. Require solid logical discipline in the formation, collection, use of, and saving of metrics results. If you do this across the organization, metrics can be "rolled up" to show how the entire organization is performing.

A journey of a thousand miles
must begin with a single step.
—*Lao Tzu*

Notice SMARTS includes Stretch. In my mind, stretch applied here means more than just working a small bit harder. It means doing something different. We are only doing this because something is not working or to capture some opportunity. Whatever we were doing is not bringing the results we seek. If we want things to be different, we have to be different.

If the challenge is too hard, like solving world hunger or climate change, these may get a lot of energy in discussion, and not much is likely to happen in the near term. The goals are just too large. On the other hand, if the challenge is too easy, like rearranging the pencils in your desk drawer, the outcome is meaningless, and few will actually work on it.

The difference between too hard and too easy is called creative tension. You can read more about this in *The Fifth Discipline: The Art & Practice of the Learning Organization* by Peter Senge et al. and online.

We are seeking just enough creative tension to entice people to work on it and setting the goal just easy enough so they believe they can make a difference, and thus, they do.

> *If you think you can, you can,*
> *and if you think you can't, you can't.*
> *—Henry Ford*

Figure 33 gives an example of how the level of stretch can be evaluated. This is a working example I developed for one of my clients. It is used in their employee evaluation system. Study this table for a few moments. Something like this can be used to evaluate tactics and how much effort and time are to be expected in order to make progress. Each project has its own characteristics, but they tend to fall into categories depending on degree of difficulty. This is a way to tease out the difficulty of one project relative to another.

Figure 33

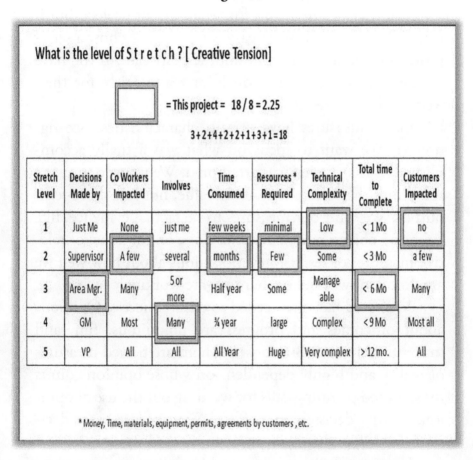

What is the level of S t r e t c h ? [Creative Tension]

= This project = 18 / 8 = 2.25

3+2+4+2+2+1+3+1=18

Stretch Level	Decisions Made by	Co Workers Impacted	Involves	Time Consumed	Resources* Required	Technical Complexity	Total time to Complete	Customers Impacted
1	Just Me	None	just me	few weeks	minimal	Low	< 1 Mo	no
2	Supervisor	A few	several	months	Few	Some	< 3 Mo	a few
3	Area Mgr.	Many	5 or more	Half year	Some	Manage able	< 6 Mo	Many
4	GM	Most	Many	¾ year	large	Complex	< 9 Mo	Most all
5	VP	All	All	All Year	Huge	Very complex	> 12 mo.	All

* Money, Time, materials, equipment, permits, agreements by customers , etc.

No two projects have the same level of stretch. You can easily take your project and see how it fits into this table.

Each project will fit differently. Your project will be defined by the questions asked across the top of the table. Your situation may call for slightly different questions across the top. Just use a highlighter for the most appropriate box in each column to place that aspect of the project on the table and to compare two or more projects in the level of stretch or creative tension present.

You may not need this for your current project, but it is useful to know there are easy ways to clarify how a set of projects stack up against one another, especially if you have to then compensate individuals or teams fairly for their work and successes.

Good measures have certain characteristics. See figure 34. We want to focus on what was actually accomplished, not just what was attempted. We want to measure the things that create long-term value, not just short-term output. We want our measures to be factual evidence, like counting objects or dollars, tasks done or not done, or relative measures of results, never opinions about how well we are doing, or worse, how hard we are working!

Measured facts are needed to ensure success. Opinions about outcomes and progress are ubiquitous, fun, and make us feel good. But most of them are flawed measures of reality and highly dependent on whose opinion counts most. Good planning calls for weeding out the use of opinions to drive decisions and effort. We want fact-based decision-making to drive our processes toward success.

For example, hard measures like dollars, time, production units, etc., are much easier to measure. In fact, at some levels, most are already available, but they are mostly only available at the back of the bus, after it is too late to make adjustments. Soft (frequently called very hard) measures are much harder to measure, but usually much more valuable as a predictor of future success.

Example lead measures might be the following:

- Employee morale (perhaps a surrogate for productivity)
- Efforts in compliance with environmental or health standards (perhaps a surrogate for incident and lawsuit avoidance)
- Ratio of sales leads to sales meetings (perhaps a surrogate for staff productivity and thus potential sales)
- Sales meetings that end in an order (perhaps a surrogate for future production demand)
- Direct contact events with customers to evaluate satisfaction (perhaps a surrogate for return buys)

Good measures have some common characteristics.

Figure 34

Characteristics of Good Measures

- Quantitative [and qualitative if the only way .. ..usually for leading indicators]

- Leading if possible and meaningful [work in progress and lagging when necessary]

- Accurate , reliable, verifiable, measured data [not opinions]

- Uncomplicated - [easy to understand the link to success]

- Key drivers of most critical behaviors to fulfill our mission and vision.

- Drives changed behaviors and outcomes [what will you do differently ?]

- Makes us think deeply about what set of routine behaviors is driving the numbers.

- Feedback on trends in time to make effective changes [no surprises]

- Ratios and or rates comparing one important indicator with another .

- Milestones accomplished , not efforts or activities [not how hard you worked – what you got done]

- Within the control of the performer

- Pass the SMARTS test

Accountability and performance increase dramatically when we have the routine behavioral discipline to set specific times and places for DOing specific tasks. We want to list specifically Who Will Do What By When.

These descriptors are the key components of personal and organizational accountability. If there are contingencies like weather, they can be handled by using ranges of time for performance, etc. The specific activities of the tactics have to actually be scheduled and then measured for this to work well.

There is a big difference between saying, "I am going to lose one pound each week" versus "On Monday, Wednesday, and Friday, after work at 5:00 p.m., I am going to the gym for one hour and have a full workout, weigh myself every day, and adjust my eating habits daily so my weight chart moves steadily in a downward trend to meet my timed goal of one pound a week for the next eight weeks," and then put that in your calendar and actually do it.

We get the best outcomes in this highly disciplined way. Structure, clarity, stability, routine, predictability, and accountability are all necessary for us to function at our highest levels. We need to make ourselves accountable for processes capable of actually producing the desired result.

Measure is the place in the **PDCA** cycle where we become accountable to one another for shared plans. If we are going to succeed, the DOing needs to be planned with specific outcomes and actions set for an agreed-upon time, by whom, etc., the Wizards and WWDWBW. We can't succeed relying on "when we get around to it," "soon," "next," or the worst of all, "I am working on it." Or even worse, not specifying who will do it or even when. These loose fuzzy commitments are direct paths to the failure of a broken **PDCA** cycle.

How will this data be used right now to improve our process and outcomes?

It works best to break the strategy down into discrete tactics of specific tasks bounded by time, outcome, and performers that are within control of the performers who have enough capacity and the commitment to make it work (WWDWBW). Then we knit together a string of these till all the tasks are done. Each completed successful step becomes a milestone to celebrate and motivate us to continue on our plan.

To their detriment, many leaders try to PLAN much more than can be implemented within the current capacity. I think they believe this is smart planning, and of course, it can look impressive at the start. This is not smart planning as it is not realistic. I think it makes us feel good to know we have a PLAN, ignoring the fact that the PLAN is not matched by capacity and thus reality.

To my mind, this is like selling something we do not own. While it is a good idea to have some PLANs ready and standing in reserve in case there is an unforeseen change in schedule and thus an opportunity of working on them and they need to be clearly identified as such, we don't want to waste important current resources on PLANs for work that is too far off in the distance. Things change too rapidly, and all that future planning could all just be wasted. Focus on what we can do now.

Stacking up huge backlog lists of tasks for people "just in case" is a real downer. Looking up at a never-ending wall of work with no clear PLAN for when it will be done is a sign of poor understanding of motivation and PLANning by the leader. More, it can drive us to just work on the huge list of projects we had already planned when perhaps reality and thus priorities should have changed to meet some new emerging reality. We might do this since it is the easy and most comfortable path when stuck on DO.

I think of this like herding cats. I can make a plan for herding 1,000 cats, but that energy is wasted if I only have enough resources to actually herd 50 cats. The time spent on the 950 others was a total waste of time. Focus on triage and what you can actually expect to DO.

It is outcomes, not effort, that are the measure of a good PLAN. Busyness is a fine excuse but not effort that builds momentum or results. We need focused behaviors that drive results. It is very common to stay busy rewriting our daily to-do list when we really ought to just be doing the number one most important item. We already know what that is. Why fool ourselves? We measure individual tasks to ensure our effort and output for the entire PLAN are on track.

I will refrain from exploring the whole important versus critical debate. We all have to do this dance every day and every moment in our lives. We just need to be sure we are triaging all the demands we face. I think those who are good at this are already well on their way to success. Those who fiddle while Rome burns won't be helped with more words from me about that.

It's a hell of a lot easier to get older than it is to get wiser.

Let's face it, some people are just not methodical or disciplined. And they don't want to be disciplined by you and your fussy planning. They just want to do what they feel like at the moment. They may be good team mates on the DO part of the project as long as their habits don't inhibit the other three steps. This may make them happy. Perhaps they need to work somewhere else since they don't belong on this team if they can't abide the full **PDCA** process.

We want to build a sense of accomplishment by keeping tasks manageable, bite-sized, within the limits of our resources, capability, influence, and thus more likely of success. Better to succeed at five small steps within our grasp than fail on one large project that could have easily been divided into five doable and successful steps. Success breeds success.

How do you eat an elephant? One bite at a time. Catch your elephants and devour them one leg at a time. And don't spend your time building big plans you may never get to. Better to just get started on the most important one now. A well-defined strategy that all agree will meet the challenge will keep you on a successful path.

> *God put me on this Earth to accomplish*
> *a certain number of things. Right now,*
> *I'm so far behind that I'll never die.*
> *—Thomas Hobbes*

I urge you to become familiar with the Premack principle. Look it up now. It says that the best way to structure our work is to always do the least desirable tasks first, followed by ever more desirable tasks, followed by even more desirable tasks. Some call this Grandma's peas. You have to eat your peas before you get ice cream.

That way we are not doing all the fun things first and giving up on doing the hard, boring, or tedious things, causing a broken **PDCA** cycle. This is not always possible, but it is important to understand we can't leave all the hard, boring, or undesirable work for last.

*If it's your job to eat a frog, it's best
to do it first thing in the morning.
And if it's your job to eat two frogs,
it's best to eat the biggest one first.*
—*Mark Twain*

This is why we need to create an entire PLAN before we start. Most people say, "I will figure out the measurements later," leaving the coordination of tasks and measures till it is too late, and we find we did the work with no meaningful measures, no measures of conditions before we started, and thus, no factual evidence-based learning from the change. This is back-of-the-bus thinking. We want to know the WWDWBW before we start so we know when we are done or that we are about to fail on our plan.

What about the Wizards and SMARTS test? Would the team leader, team members, and stakeholders agree the list of tasks for this tactic pass the test? If your answers are all yes, congratulations. If not, re-cycle iteratively back through the wizards and SMARTS tests till all stakeholders agree the list of tasks are going to make this effort a success and they are the best list available.

It usually takes a few tweaks to get all of a PLAN right. Surprisingly, usually, all that is needed is changing or melding of some terms to get alignment since our language is so fraught with confused meaning, and simple alternative words are all that is needed. Go back to figure 18 and look at all the similar words we use to describe our work. The work is the same, but we each have our favorite words. Differences over a PLAN are frequently just terminology issues. Perhaps you have been to the meeting where two people argued for an hour only to discover they wanted the same thing but used different words to describe it.

We are targeting an 80–20 level of agreement here, not perfect, forever, life-or-death alignment. Again, if you are not familiar with the 80–20 rule, look up the "Pareto Principle" on the internet. We need a good PLAN to get moving. Learning and process improvement only occurs when we actually test our PLAN against a real-world challenge.

PLANS are usually developed in offices or meeting rooms, and the learning usually starts when we actually get up and go out to test our PLAN in the real world. A reasonably good PLAN fully implemented is much, much better than a perfect PLAN too complicated or delayed by pursuit of perfection.

Before you start to build measures, I suggest you create a metrics tree for your system. If you are not familiar with this idea, look it up now. See figure 35. It shows the beginnings of a tree for the factors that make up earnings. There are many other examples on the internet. Your need for a measure may not be economic as shown here, but the example holds.

Once you decide what factor you want to change, you will be better at it if you understand what drives that factor. The most powerful way to do this is to convene the people who are working on this and ask them to build a metrics tree chart like this for the process in question. They will have a diversity of opinions and usually disagree about what elements are the most important. Great, we rarely learn much from those who easily agree with us.

***We don't get harmony when
everybody sings the same note.***

*Only notes that are different
can harmonize.
The same is true with people.*
　　　　　　　—Steve Goodier

This discussion time is very useful as it brings more focus on the underlying processes, and it creates an opportunity for the very people who affect these outcomes to more fully understand how what they do affect all the others and the end result. You can find many examples of metrics trees on the internet.

Figure 35

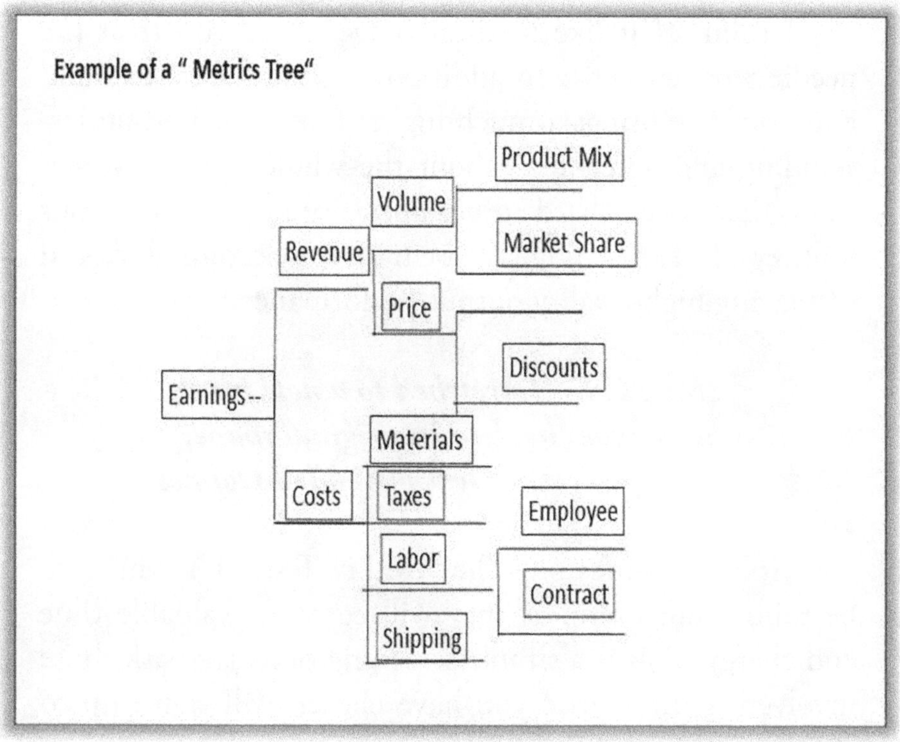

Example of a " Metrics Tree"

- Earnings--
  - Revenue
    - Volume
      - Product Mix
      - Market Share
    - Price
      - Discounts
  - Costs
    - Materials
    - Taxes
    - Labor
      - Employee
      - Contract
    - Shipping

A metrics tree can help you and all involved in the creation of a shared mental model for how your system creates value and results. Most people can relate to the big outcomes like revenue and cost but are not so good and fully understanding how those actually come about.

We need to find out where the big-leverage items are. You can't measure everything. A metrics tree improves focus on the most important factors now. Think about which of the above metrics would be lagging and which would be work in progress or even better leading. Once you have a metrics tree, you will be better at choosing what most needs attention at this time. We want to be influencing the root of our problems, not the simple, on-the-surface manifestation of it.

I think of it like medical triage where you treat the neediest patient first. In addition, a group effort to build a metrics tree brings a much higher level of shared under-standing and agreement about the whole process, some-thing that is very hard to get and very important on our journey of (1) learning, (2) being more accountable, and (3) having high-quality output/performance.

> *Man's mind stretched to a new idea*
> *never goes back to its original shape.*
> *—Oliver Wendell Holmes*

Good measures pass the "Reality Test." They need to be robust and useful as they will consume valuable time and energy. This is a simple screening process to ask those involved if the metric you have chosen will stand up to its use to drive results. Metrics may be useful to leaders, but remember, they will drive the behaviors of those whose activities and behaviors are critical to outcomes.

> *The front line drives the bottom line.*
> *Set up metrics that are*
> *inspiring to the front line.*

Be sure those impacted know that your goal is (1) learning, (2) accountability, and (3) higher overall performance. Be sure they know this is not about fixing blame; it is about fixing the problem. It is about creating a system where the old problem simply no longer exists because we are now better than we used to be; we grew our way out of that problem by being smarter than we were. The organization needs to know where changes are needed so everyone can succeed. See figure 36.

You want accountability that drives success, not just marking off time spent or efforts put forth, but results obtained that lead to the goal. So not just keeping score as in lag measures, but repeating the behaviors that run up the score as in lead measures.

Figure 36

The Reality Test	
Can your plan and intended metrics pass this test ?	
Specific	Clearly tells Who Will Do What By When
Controllable	Within your power to control the outcomes
Facts	Actual measured and documented results, no impressions, opinions , or guesses
Data	Counts, flows, rates, ratios, discreet values , that is logged , charted, and saved
Reliable	Three or more observers would agree on the measured results and outcome

The Creator gave us imagination
so we could dream up the vision of
the future and then strive to reach
it, and a sense of humor to live with
our selves while on the journey.
—Unknown

Don't be put off by the natural variability that occurs in measurement when the results fluctuate. Think trend and direction. Frequent measurements accumulated over time will begin to show the normal amount of variability to expect. Just be sure things are steadily headed in the right direction.

Good metrics are hard to create. It takes time and trial and error. We want to use a CASA approach to building metrics that are more leading than lagging and more standardized than unique. I recommend you do the best you can to create several of each type (leading, work in progress, and lagging) and monitor them over some specific preplanned time. Then when that time is up, ask what you learned about variability and trends and how can you improve each of the metrics you have in place. Ahhhh, **PDCA!**

We can't measure much in this complex world. There is just not enough time. We need to be focused on selecting measures that are the most likely to bring about future success. It is easy to dream up more things to measure. I recommend you spend a big chunk of your time paring down the number of metrics and embracing more of the ones you believe will bring about success.

The fact that something has already been set up and measured for years in interesting, but it may not be important. Take a look at figure 37. It may be helpful in deciding which current metrics you want to discard in favor of more powerful compelling things to measure.

Now let's talk about how to share measured results. Numbers are good, but graphic displays are much, much better. Take a look at figure 38.

We humans are really good at digesting information in graphic form. A few of us are good at digesting tables of numbers, but most are not. We want results to be impactful to drive the behaviors we need. Graphic results are the gold standard for display of measures. Three-quarters of our neurons are associated with vision. Telling is good, but seeing is much, much better.

Once a metric has been developed, I suggest you keep it front and center in every discussion about the work and progress on the metric. Good metrics are not just numbers, they are graphs. Graphs allow for much more rapid and effective assimilation of the information. They tell a story of past, present, trend, and thus perhaps the future. They show scale of performance over time. We will be working on development of useful graphs in the next chapter.

A picture is worth a thousand words, and a map is worth a thousand pictures.

Figure 37

Measurement Considerations

Consider	The Questions:
Exists	Are measures already available? Use them.
Method	Check List, log, report, data sheet, forms, extract from monthly report?
Scale	Time frame [days, years,] and units [$, hrs., reports, forms] ?
What	Behavior [Work in Progress, or Lead] or output [Lag] to measure – specifically ?
Where	Locations to measure and record and share
When	Start, end, frequency?
Why	Objective of the measure?
How	Collect, summarize, report, create and post chart of results?
Who	The performer[s] or perhaps some other process?
How Much	Collect data for a while. Analyze it. Decide if you need to change the measure. Then repeat. Watch for trends. PDCA the process till you get what you need. This is continuous process improvement.

From a leadership point of view, culturally, the most important thing about measuring performance is that the outcome must be used to learn, improve, and advance performance
and NEVER TO PUNISH OR EMBARRASS!

Figure 38

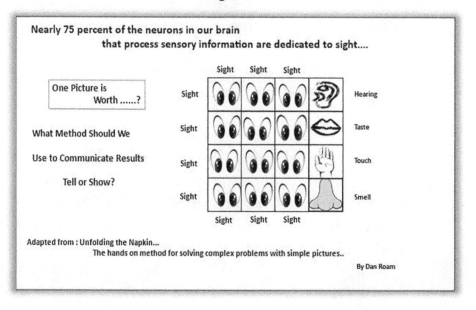

Don't keep your metrics chart in a binder or on some back shelf. Put it up on the wall in a prominent place where all the performers can see it. If it is important, it deserves a prominent display. I bet there is a clock in some prominent place at your work. Your important metric needs as much attention as a clock.

When you sit with people to talk about projects or their work performance, keep the chart front and center on the desk between you, turned toward them. Use it as a springboard for the discussion of what is planned, what is happening, and what has happened so far (Lead, WIP, and Lag indicators). Make the discussion about the measured facts that are emerging.

Why not? You are both trying to bring about new outcomes as shown on the chart. Teach them by your example that you are committed to using measurement to discover facts and efforts that drive performance.

Facts are our friends. Let's
find 'em and use 'em!

They will take their cues from you. If you routinely refer to it to discuss progress and their efforts, they will know you are serious about using measured facts to improve learning, accountability, and performance. Better yet, show them some metric where you show by example how your own work is measured and charted.

People don't do what you expect,
they do what you inspect.
—Monica Cornetti

Finally, I want to share a way of challenging ourselves when creating plans called the 4 *M*s. It is not enough to simply measure things. You have to do more. You have to effectively use those time-consuming measurement efforts to make changes that bring you closer to your vision. The 4 *M*s can be useful to remind us more is needed. The *M*s stand for the following: M1 = measure, M2 = monitor, M3 = manage, and M4 = mentor. These are key steps to success and all are important for long term success. They are simple to learn and use. See figure 39.

It would be easy to dismiss the 4 *M*s, but they can be a powerful way of ensuring we have thought all this through. The best PLAN in the world is useless if it is not practical and easy to use. In the next chapter, I will show an example of how all this fits together.

I think the most powerful is M4. Without leadership behaviors showing the way and mentoring others, people will do what they think is best, and frequently, that is not well aligned with what is best for the organization. That is the role of the leader.

Figure 39

The 4 M's in Action

M	Effort	Questions
M 1	Lead Measure	What early actions would best lead us to success ?
M 1	WIP	What work in progress data documents that we are on our plan ?
M 1	Lag Measure	What end result would best show our success ?
M 2	Monitor	How we actually monitor this flow of data for best effectiveness
M 3	Manage	What do we need to be doing right now to keep us on plan ?
M 4	Mentor	How will I show the others by example the path to success ?

Chapter Summary

This chapter expanded more on DO, the second step of **PDCA**, by exploring how to use Measures to follow and ensure things get done as planned.

This chapter contained a number of different ways of looking carefully at something to be measured. Included here are more of these tools than you would need or use regularly. My intent was to share multiple frameworks with the intent some of them will help you. Do not be put off by the apparent redundancy.

Without effective measures, how would you know what is really going on? Figure 40 gives some truths about the value of measurement.

Figure 40

Value of Measurement	
Without Measurement	
Performance can't be managed	Decisions are based on opinion , guesses , or worse
People won't know if their efforts and performance is on track	There is no fact based foundation for rewards or correction
There are no fact based triggers for process improvement	People can't know what is expected of them , exactly
The organization fails to build The discipline of performance	Individuals can easily waste time And resources without consequence

Finally and most importantly for leaders, metrics give us a sense of progress. Many studies have shown that if there is no sense of progress, it is much too easy to lose commitment to the work.

Now let's move on to working some specific metrics examples.

CHAPTER 9

— ⁂ —

DO: 6) Measure—Specific Examples

Chapter Summary

This chapter expands on the prior chapter. It takes us from general thoughts about metrics to how to actually build some metrics. We will now return to our selected example and work up some BOTs for it and several other examples.

First, to set the stage for understanding what is to come, let's have some fun with some funny metrics. Let's make up a metric about Mr. Skinny Smith. Skinny likes doughnuts, and he likes to make people jealous. He has a hard time staying on track with PLANs. Perhaps you know him?

Skinny took some time to carefully chart out his PLAN to gain twenty-five pounds in three months. He read this book and finally mastered all this alphabet soup jargon and spent some CASA thinking time about how **PDCA**, the Wizards, WWDWBW, SMARTS, the 4 *M*s, and M V V S

T M L N could help clarify his PLAN. Here is his current thinking. Please carefully study figure 41 as it pulls together much of what we have talked about till now. I know this chart is congested and hard to read. Read it anyway. Find each of the elements we have been covering. Then see how Skinny filled in the chart with his PLAN.

What if you had a blank chart like this for the next time you begin to make a plan? Well, you do now as there is a blank chart like this waiting for you in appendix A. You may have to modify it a bit to make it work for you. I do think these CASA tools force you to be concise, a prerequisite for any good plan.

Notice how **PDCA**, the Wizards, SMARTS, the 4 *M*s, and M V V S T M L N are arrayed around the chart. They may not map directly in sequence as they were explained when presented earlier, but they are all here in Skinny's plan.

Values do not map very clearly in this example unless you consider accuracy, persistence, timeliness, transparency, and dedication values. I do, and they are embedded but not really stated separately in his PLAN. If a PLAN is good enough, the values are embedded and easy to detect.

Figure 41

PDCA , Wizards , SMARTS, 4 M , WWDWBW, MVVSTMLN Work Sheet Name *Skinny Smith*   Start Date *Today* *Mission*

P L A N

What **S**pecific = Measure - I will : *Gain 25 pounds in 3 months by eating 5 doughnuts daily*

Who   *I will do this all by myself*   WWDWBW   *Vision*

Where   *In my truck, at home, at the doughnut shop , at Starbucks , etc.*

Measureable =   *Measure*

D O

How   Measure = M 1 = Lag MEASURE :   *Measure and log / plot my weight every day*

Much   = M 1 = Lead MEASURE :   *Count and log Number of doughnuts eaten daily*

Monitor = M 2 = I will MONITOR by : *Charting / posting lead / lag data at my desk weekly*

Manage = M 3 = I will MANAGE by : *Share plan PUBLICLY and follow it persistently*

C H

Mentor = M 4 = I will MENTOR by :   *Showing others how to use the tools to be successful* *Strategy*

E C K

How **A**chievable = this is within my control : *I can do this , it is just up to me; and I love doughnuts*

I will overcome the obstacles of: *Focusing on other things, & fear of the jelly filled monsters,* *Tactics*

by : *doing this by noon each day* and : *smashing the jelly filled monsters before I eat them*

Why **R**elevant = drives my lag measure of: *Gain 25 pounds to make others jealous of my success* *Values*

A D J U S T

When **T**imed = Start : *Tuesday* with feedback check ins with : *My Manager* and *My spouse* *Learning*

in *3 weeks* and *6 weeks* and in *3 months* till this becomes a habit

Make adjustments to the plan after each check in if needed to ensure success

How **S**tretch = *Practice new behavior consistently* Requiring CASA : *dedication*

persistence, [and bigger pants] for me, which I can master and use on my next project *Next*

Skinny wanted to share his results with his coworkers, so he worked up a Behavior Over Time (BOT) graph to show his PLAN and progress. See figure 42. He posted this above his desk where he and everyone else could see it. Then he worked the PLAN every day, weighed himself every day, ate at least five doughnuts every day, and gradually posted the results.

Plan your work, and work your plan.
—Napoleon Hill

Gradually, over the three plus months, Skinny achieved his goal of gaining twenty-five pounds and more. The dashed wavy trend line shows his weight varying but gradually climbing to twenty-five pounds and more above his starting weight. Then near the end of the third month, he cut back on doughnuts, and his weight moderated.

Figure 42

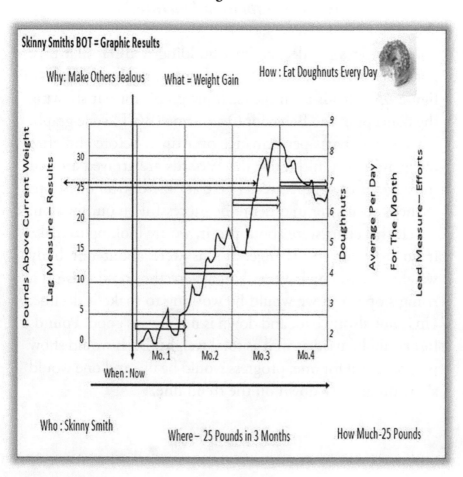

This is quite a simple BOT to construct, especially if you are making it from the worksheet shown on figure 41. Think of how you might be able to use this approach to quantify the results you need to reach your vision.

One picture is worth 1,000 words,
and a clear BOT, like a good map,
is worth a thousand pictures!

Now let's go deeper into building a BOT like this. Let's start with the basic BOT framework shown here in figure 43. This is a simple example graph format showing the concept of the Behavior Over Time (BOT) style graph. This graph charts performance over time, before and after our plan is begun. Notice the Wizards are arrayed around the edge of the graph area. These are the critical questions we need to answer in order to be successful on our mission.

If this chart were about profit, we are looking to make it go up after the change. If this were about our body weight, we might have a chart where the trend was on a rising slope, and we would be working to make it decline. Up is not always bad, and down is not always good. Pounds lost could be used as well as total weight. Both would show progress, and for one, progress would be up, and one would show progress as down on the trend line.

Figure 43

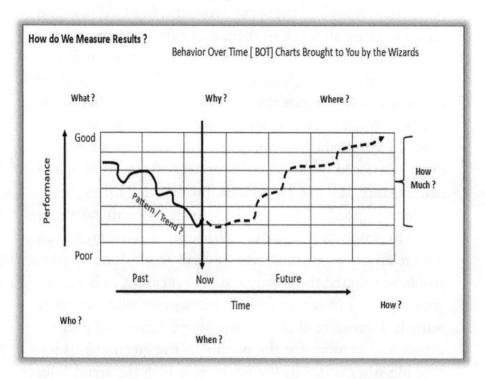

Most people start to make a graph with Now at the left end of the time axis. I always start by showing a bit of the past since something in the past drove us to want to make some changes and this graph in the first place. We are in the present at Now, but need to be altering or building on the past.

Let's face it, we are rarely ever at the beginning of any story. This issue and our current position are a function of all that went on before. We can't ignore the past, and we want to find a way to use that to build a better future.

Our current position at Now needs to be the place where we are hoping to see the start of a change occur. This would be our inflection point if we are successful. The

Wizards make it easier to identify the key considerations. Sometimes not all of them are pertinent, but CASA would have us asking all seven of them every time anyway.

Figure 43 shows that trend lines can be up or down, and time periods can be whatever you need. We are looking for patterns and trends, not absolute numbers. While both time and performance scales can be whatever set of numbers you need, I recommend you opt for simple whole numbers. For time, this could be anywhere from seconds to decades. For performance, it could be pounds, profit, tons, barrels, sales, products shipped—whatever it is you are trying to influence.

The important trends or patterns will emerge even with relatively crude measures. If clear trends don't emerge, you have selected the wrong result to measure. It is easy to get caught up in trying for precision while what we really want is a measure that tells the story. Leave the decimal points and pennies for the people in the green eyeshades. The big story is not in the pennies; it is in the trend lines after the inflection point. Where are we headed?

If a BOT measures the right things, it will tell you when you are on track and when you need to make adjustments in approach or rate. I like the fact that it points to past, present, and future. It is much more like a movie than a snapshot. It is very hard to communicate complex relationships with text or a verbal description that can be instantly understood with a BOT. BOTs let us use our natural visual skills to instantly understand the relationships and results so we can spend more time discussing the "So what" questions.

What if you had a blank chart like this to use to build your next PLAN? Well, relax, you have a blank BOT chart like this waiting for you in appendix B.

Remember the 4 *Ms*? Once you decide to commit resources to improve something, you will be thinking about how to Measure, Monitor, Manage, and Mentor it. A measurement plan without these key ingredients is a PLAN to struggle and fail. The BOT chart will make all those much easier. I see this as the core solution. Once you are committed to action, this is your path.

Now let's take our previous working example and build some measures. Figure 44 shows figure26 over again for tactic 4b from chapter 7 transferred here as a refresher.

Figure 44
This is Figure 26 from Chapter 7.
Second Set of Tactics for Strategy Statement 4

4 b) Study the process and past 3 years of error rework to identify best opportunities

Tactic	Step	Tasks to be completed on time within the larger schedule	Process Owner
4 b	1	Identify field and office processes to be improved by gathering and studying error rates by type for past three years	Team Lead
	2	Select highest frequency error types to improve efficiency by 20%	Team
	3	Make improvements to processes to reduce errors	Team
	4	Estimate rework time savings in payroll and field offices	Team

Figure 45 shows these same 4b tactic steps re-cast against the Wizards. This table makes the tactics list clearer. It is an intermediate step to creating a graphic. Most of the time, this intermediate step would not be necessary for those with experience. I have included it here to make it easier for you to see how to use the Wizards to make developing a graphic easier. Note I have added step 5 to show this needs to be completed on time. That is shown on the table title line identifying the tasks.

Figure 45

Example Behavior Over Time Performance Schedule							
Step	What	Where	When	Why	How	Who	How Much
1	Identify field and office processes to be improved	Office	Weeks 1 & 2	Lower costs	Study error rates by type	Team Lead	Last 3 Years
2	Select errors to reduce	Office	Week 3	Improve accuracy	Focus on high frequency errors	Team	By 20%
3	Make process improvements	Office	Weeks 4,5,6	Improve efficiency	Eliminate most common errors in process	Team	Improve by 20%
4	Estimate rework time	Office	Week 7	Clarify the size of the prize	Calculate labor saved	Team	By 20 %
5	Completed on time	Office	Week 8	On Schedule within the larger strategy	Focus on schedules	Team Lead	-

In this specific example, "Where" doesn't matter since this will all be done in the office. But in other cases, it might matter. If you get in the habit of asking and documenting all seven Wizard questions each time, you will be less likely to miss important information next time. Think CASA!

Remember, this is the chance to build shared understanding and alignment, so getting those involved and impacted by an emerging PLAN is very important. If you expect support in making changes, having the key stakeholders involved in creating the PLAN is critical.

This is the essence of CASA; we use all of our tools so we don't miss critical information this time or any time. Think about the airline pilot on your next flight. You hope he has the discipline to check all the items on the preflight checklist, even if some of them don't matter this particular time. The Wizards won't ask every possible question, and the answers can sometimes require more work to be sure they are focused on the entire process. At least the Wizards improve our chances of success.

Disagreement about the table content and meaning, if conducted with positive reinforcing learning behaviors, leads to a deeper understanding of each other's views and thus the issue: always a good thing. It is much better to get differences of understanding ironed out now than after we are three weeks into some expensive PLAN. We learn most when we discuss differences rather than agreements. We can also display the same information in a step-by-step progress schedule. See figure 46.

***Be confident enough to act on the best
knowledge you have now, Humble***

*enough to doubt what you know, and
wise enough to face the hard facts when
new—better—evidence comes along.
—Pfeffer and Sutton*

Figure 46

Example Progress Schedule				
Step	Task	Statements of Progress	Type of Measure	Cumulative Score
1	Identify Processes	Process and error studies complete with schedule	Yes or No	20 %
2	Select errors	Error types leading to 20% improvement selected	Yes or No	20 + 20 = 40%
3	Improve Processes	Process improvements made	Yes or No	20+20+20 = 60%
4	Estimate Time	Savings estimated	Yes or No	20+20+20+20 = 80%
5	Completed on time	Phase 4 b completed on schedule	Yes or No	20+20+20+20+ 20 = 100%

This shows the same general information displayed on a simple "Step by Step" table. Notice the statements of progress are all stated in past tense. Using past tense will force us to acknowledge when something is actually done rather than still being worked on.

We want to be very clear what steps are done, completely done! And the score we might attach for measuring progress is not earned until the progress statement can truthfully be answered as totally complete. Thus, this is a yes or no table. As you progress down the list of steps, you keep adding points in the cumulative score column at the right till your score for this total effort adds to 100% when the project is complete.

In your own work, you may need to assign more appropriate score points for each step based on degree of difficulty. Not all five steps are likely of equal difficulty. That's fine; that can come once you can apply this to your own work. This is just a simple example.

We want to convert the text in this table into a graphic to keep track of our progress and make the work and gradually accumulating progress more compelling for those who are actually doing the work. Besides, graphs are a much more effective way of integrating all the information available to us. A graphic BOT is like a simplified Gantt or PERT chart. If you are not familiar with those tools, I urge you to look them up. See figure 47.

This is quite simple once you do it several times. The first time is the hardest. This is just an example, but most metrics for a given tactic are not more complicated than this.

This is a simple, easy way to make a BOT graphic that shows each task in relation to the others. It makes clear the dependency of each step on the one before. It shows how delays in one step cascade to all remaining steps. It shows how the tasks are divided up into discrete smaller steps nestled in the larger tactic. And it shows a ___% complete score as the series of steps moves forward.

This BOT chart shows the weeks of this set of tasks across the bottom, but could show hours, days, months, or actual dates. It shows the tasks up the left side with arrows pointing to the text of the tasks themselves. It shows the

Wizards for the tactic 4b around the edges. Look for them now; it will help you see how easy this kind of chart is to make once you understand the wisdom of the Wizards.

Figure 47

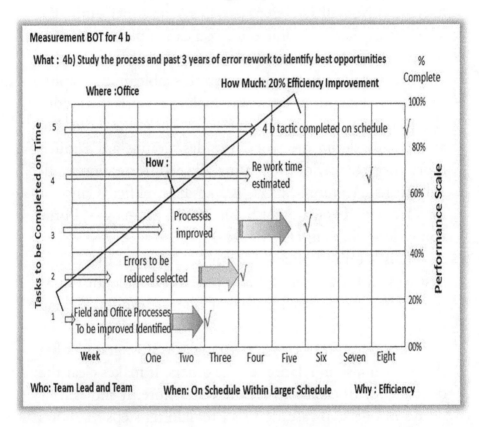

The large check marks are when each task is to be done at the end of the designated week. The large horizontal arrows show the time period when the work is actually being done. The ends of each large horizontal arrow show when it was started and ended. The pointed end is the milestone of progress for that particular effort. The Who is shown as the team lead and team. If possible, I would add the initials of each person tasked with each substep. The goal is to create ownership and accountability for the steps for everyone involved.

W W D W B W

The BOT graphic is a good way to keep everyone updated on the whole set of tasks and each individual person's part. It is also a great way to provide positive reinforcement for those whose tasks are on time. Celebrate success as often as you can.

In this example, the large horizontal arrows on the first three tasks indicate which tasks are complete or underway. The absence of large horizontal arrows for the other tasks means that those tasks have not started yet, but they are looming in the near future, so get ready. The check marks show when each task was initially scheduled to be completed.

On the right side of the chart, I show the performance score as ___% complete. As each task is completed, you can report your percent completion. With this, you can compare this to other projects and keep track of whether this project is on track compared to your overall plan. Just be sure when you say something is compete, it is entirely complete. A lack of discipline on this point leads to projects that are never complete marked as complete. This then leads to a lack of focus on the next project since this task will continue to require effort. The word *complete* should mean something!

COMPLETE = DONE = No lingering details!

Make this a cultural standard leading to new levels of accountability and performance. Do this yourself for your own work and teach it by example. Accountability 101!

Next, I show a totally unrelated example. This one is from a landscape company employee who is trying to master how to program irrigation controllers. I offer it as an example from a completely different world just to show this can easily be adapted to most anything. See figure 48.

If our tactic, and thus the strategy, is slipping, in time, a comparison of the horizontal arrows and the check marks will show by how far. If major unanticipated developments mean the PLAN and chart need to be re-cast, then working together, everyone agrees the chart milestones can be altered, but only by group agreement and the person this team leader reports to, presumably our customer, for this work.

People do what the boss inspects—
review the BOTs together.

Also, there is intense pressure when you were responsible for a task that is now delayed and thus delaying everyone else. The BOT makes this painfully clear for everyone. If someone else slips behind and you are not inclined to give them any slack or help, be prepared for the retribution coming when you fall behind. A great outcome is when others offer to help out to keep the entire process on track. Our overall goal is (1) learning, (2) accountability, and (3) quality high performance.

Figure 48

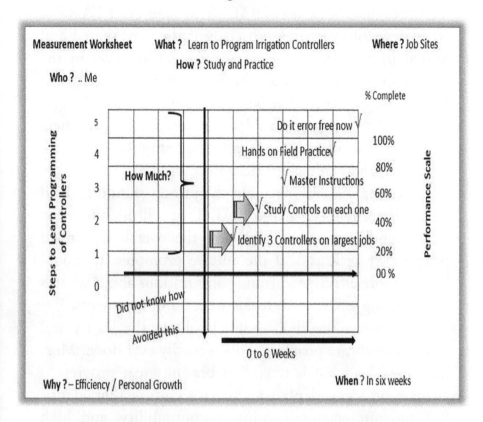

When multiple people have their hand on team success and can see how their work fits to build collective success, there is psychological pressure on each to do their part to keep the whole team on schedule.

> *An eye for an eye, and the*
> *whole world goes blind.*
> *—Mahatma Gandhi*

Many people fail to capture the huge value of converting action lists of tasks to BOTs. BOTs put our PLANS in clear view for everyone, especially if they are shared and posted prominently. They make the information in the list instantly available since the brain can rapidly grasp the facts in graphic form. The best use of this chart is to hang it on the wall in a prominent place so everyone can see where we are on the project, which tasks are complete, which are next, and when and where delays occurred.

Meeting discussions about the project should be held while all are looking at the BOT. That will highlight the accountability to each other and the overall continued progress we seek and, if the culture promotes it, should lead to more effective learning conversations about what is going wrong and how to make process improvements.

Reviewing the BOT publicly allows the leader and team to celebrate progress. This is hardly ever done. Most just press for what is next. Celebrating great progress is all part of a grand plan to build a culture that identifies and appreciates learning, accountability, and high performance.

And if there are delays or other problems, the culture really matters. Remember, if you can't talk about it, you can't fix it. In the end, smooth learningful dialogue will lead to higher levels of performance. In good PLAN reviews, all attention is turned to the PLAN on the BOT graph, not just some individual, so all energy is focused on how it all fits together, and how one player or more may need to step up becomes painfully obvious to them.

This approach is also a logic check on our planning process. If we as a team create so many tasks that none will be done on time, having a BOT for each in front of everyone in team meetings should drive us to be more realistic in our estimates of what we can actually tackle at any one time. This realization is part of our system capacity building.

While the BOTs seem to make individuals more accountable for their part, a full set of them drive all of us, especially leaders, to be more rational about what we can actually take on at one time. We need to be accountable for the allocation of our limited resources and priorities. It takes discipline to want to operate this way, the CASA discipline of learning, accountability, and performance. This example using a simple yes/no chart makes it easy to see if we are on track and how each of the tasks of the tactic are moving over time.

Finally, and I think most importantly, many see these simple charts as not being meaningful. They just look too easy and simple to be important. Some might be tempted to make metric charts look more complex and thus somehow more impressive. We are not trying to impress anyone with these; we are trying to make them very quick and easy to make, understand, and most importantly, follow.

Most leaders do understand the schedule since they make them. They do understand the steps since they listed them or lead that effort. They understand the progress since they sweat this out daily. They know all this, so they assume those responsible for implementation do as well. Our goal is learning, accountability, and performance, which flow from simple compelling metrics charts.

Most failures are not lack of motivation; they are failures of knowing exactly what to do and why. People want to do good work. People want to meet the challenges they face. So do you! But lack of clear direction leads to a high percentage of process failures.

BOT charts are a way of making all this very clear in one simple effective graphic you can use to lead discussions on project PLANS and outcomes. You can collectively use the BOT to build the PLAN, and you can use the BOT to accomplish the PLAN.

Now take a look at figure 49. It is a chart I worked up to show how the PLAN chart would look for a completely different situation. I have included it here to show how some other PLAN might look. It is about a leader who needs to be better at leading and coaching subordinates. This is a common need in organizations, perhaps in yours?

Study it carefully to see how it fits the situation. Look to see if it tells WWDWBW? Look to see how it satisfies the eight steps of Mission, Vision, Values, Strategy, Tactics, Measures, Learning, and Next. How does it satisfy the 4 *Ms*? What are the metrics? As you get better at this, checking for the key elements of a great PLAN will get easier.

Figure 49

PAP	Name _Mystery Emerging Leader_	Start Date _Start Date_	More detail on reverse	

P L A N

What — Specific = Lead Measure .. I will :_Spend 10 min/wk. in one-on-one's to track and coach EE performance_ _Mission_

Who — _With each member of my team_

Where — _At an appropriate effective setting_ _Vision_

DO CHECK

Measureable =

How Much —
- Measure = M 1 = Lag Measure : _Accountability culture_
- = Lead MEASURE : _10 min. one-on-one EE sessions / wk - Log and chart my efforts daily_
- Monitor = M 2 = I will MONITOR by : _By charting and posting my results over my desk weekly_ _Measure_
- Manage = M 3 = I will MANAGE by : _Sharing my plan PUBLICLY and then doing it persistently_
- Mentor = M 4 = I will learn , improve , be an example... Teach and MENTOR others to do the same

How — Achievable = this is within my control / influence : _I can do this , it is just up to me_ _Strategy_
I will overcome the obstacles of : _Focusing on other things_, and : _My fear of the unknown conflicts_ .
by _doing this by noon each day ...._ and _facing my fears – I am the boss and I need to lead_ _Tactics_

Why — Relevant = this influences my / our lag measure goal of ; _Increasing accountability in our_
team, and expect to then spend less time _problem solving due to better skills, guidance, etc._ _Values_

ADJUST

When — Timed = Start : _This Tuesday_ with feedback check ins with :_My Manager_ and _Each Team Member_ in
3 weeks and _12 weeks_ and i n _6 months_ [enter actual dates] till this becomes habit _Learning_
and make adjustments to the plan after each check in if needed to ensure success

How — Stretch = This plan means I / we have to: _Practice a new behavior consistently_ .. Which is a stretch requiring:
dedication , persistence, and humility from me / us.   **PDCA in Action !** _Next_

Now, back to our main track. Let's take one tactic from our working project list from above. We want to select which type of errors to work to correct. See figure 50.

The key here is to keep a log of the errors that require correction and how much time goes into the corrections. This means logging the corrections as they are made so we know what types of errors are most common. Many don't bother to do this. Then you have no data, thus, no facts to guide you in where to make the most effective improvements.

Figure 50

Example Progress Schedule

4b) Study the process and past 3 years of error rework to identify best opportunities

Step	Task	Statements of Progress	Type of Measure	Cumulative Score
2	Select Errors	Error types leading to 20 % efficiency improvement selected	Yes or No	20 + 20 = 40%

Once we have a log of error corrections, we want to analyze which are the most prevalent and time-consuming. I have made up a simple dummy list here in figure 51 as an example. This intentionally very short sample is just to give you insight to the types of analysis to use.

This is only shown as an example for clarity. In reality, such a table might include hundreds of lines of data. You can easily make similar logs for whatever problem you are trying to solve. Remember, in this case, we are looking to reduce errors by 20 percent in the time-reporting system. Analyzing this kind of data should lead us to some simple conclusions about how to get the savings we are looking for.

After studying an actual log of errors, say over the past six months or year, you should see patterns. For example, there are no errors for the Eastern Division. This tells me the basic system works because it works there. You may also notice most of the errors are from the Western Division. This helps us identify where to put our focus, energy, and resources. This is easy to see here by eye. In a much larger file of data, you would want to do a Pareto analysis on the number of errors from each division and perhaps even for the correction time.

Figure 51

Time Reporting Errors During February				
Date	From #	Form %	Type &	Minutes to Correct
2/3	W	56230	L	22
2/4	W	56480	E	8
2/4	S	63222	I	15
2/5	W	89255	M	33
2/7	S	35666	L	15
2/9	N	22560	L	22
2/9	W	56944	L	18
2/12	W	56988	M	25
2/14	N	64255	I	22
2/16	W	57809	E	22

# = From W = Western Division   % = Payroll form record   & = L = Late
     S = Southern Division   E = math errors
     N = Northern Division   I = illegible
     E = Eastern Division   M = missing

If you are not familiar with Pareto analysis, it is easy to do. Look that up now. What if you noticed the errors were mostly where this function is only performed part-time by staff who have other primary duties? That might help isolate the focus of the solution.

So if the leading issue is errors, the solution is probably lack of skill, thus training. If the leading issue is forms arriving late, then the solution is probably lack of knowing what to do, clear instructions. Usually the patterns in the data are obvious.

> **You can observe a lot, just by watching**
> **—Yogi Berra**

Once you have identified a high-potential leverage point it's time to ask the five whys.

Five Why's Example:
Time reporting system errors

> *THE FIRST WHY. Persistent errors require costly time interacting with the field to make corrections needed to ensure payroll system is accurate.*

> *THE SECOND WHY. Most common errors occur in the Western Division.*

> *THE THIRD WHY. The position of time-reporting clerks in the Western Division has seen unfortunate high and persistent*

turnover. New clerks only last about three weeks. They are there just long enough to get proficient when they leave for better pay.

THE FOURTH WHY. The market of clerical positions is hot in the Western Division territory since many financial support firms have relocated there in the past eight years to take advantage of clients in the area.

THE FIFTH WHY. Our pay structures are common across all divisions in all company locations. The Western Division is in a much hotter labor market, yet is constrained by the company's pay system, which holds all jobs to a common pay structure, thus high turnover and thus high errors.

Questions:

Q1: What was the original mindset? The problem was just sloppy work that could be corrected with clearer direction or training.

Q2: Could this outcome have been avoided? How? Regular monitoring (logging and analysis of errors—think 4 *M*s) would have highlighted issues in the Western Division sooner, leading to more timely corrective action once the five whys helped us find the root cause.

Oh, we could descend on all the company time-reporting offices with mandates for better accuracy. Or we could even focus on the Western Division and insist the errors stop, or heads would roll. Or we could find that we need to do something about the salary structure in the Western Division. Which of these is easiest? Which of these is most likely to solve the problem?

It's a trick, the easy way
out leads back in.

What if the five whys had discovered some other explanation?

- A supervisor was not staffing the time-reporting position adequately.
- Western Division time-reporting clerks were never trained.
- Western Division reporting requirements were different and more complex than the rest in the company, and the existing system allowed no place to report special circumstances. Clerks were trying to use a system that did not allow accuracy, so they did the best they could.

We could go on and on. The five whys may be your best friend going forward in your pursuit of learning, accountability, and performance. It's always best to solve the root problem rather than its surface manifestation.

Once the primary sources of error are known, we can construct a BOT PLAN to improve the situation. I have created one here for the case of the high turnover in the Western Division time-reporting function.

See figure 52. This PLAN takes six months but should solve the problem. In the meantime, some special accommodation will be needed in the Western Division to ensure accurate payroll. This should be a much more effective solution than just demanding that the errors stop across all offices.

The 7 Wizards are arrayed around the body of the chart. This BOT is shown as if the project is underway for two and a half months. The tasks are numbered on the left axis and called out on those lines. The percent complete standings are shown on the right axis.

Now to tie this all together, here is an eight-step way to look at this particular issue:

1. Mission—Reduce time-reporting errors, reassign staff
2. Vision—Errors reduced by 20 percent, staff reassigned
3. Values—Root cause, accuracy, thorough, timely
4. Strategy—Adjust salaries, reduce turnover, reassign staff
5. Tactics—Study salaries and adjust, train clerks, check results
6. Measures—Log errors, use BOTs to monitor errors and project learning
7. Next—Team success, team learning, process improvement, mission accomplished, on to the next challenge

Figure 52

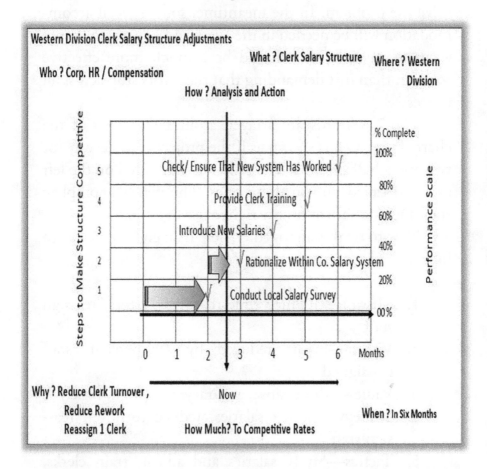

Now take a look at figure 53. It is a BOT showing the actual error data expected if this project were successful. Assuming that you now have an ongoing log of time-reporting errors, this chart would be easy to make. It reports the actual errors over time. If, as time passes, the expected results fail to begin to appear, you can watch the trend and make real-time adjustments.

Perhaps there is some new or unexpected driver your PLAN failed to see. Studying trends as they emerge is your way to keep things on track. This function needs a WIP metric. Ask yourself if you are measuring leading or lagging indicators. Recast your metrics to capture the measure most likely to lead to success.

Figure 53

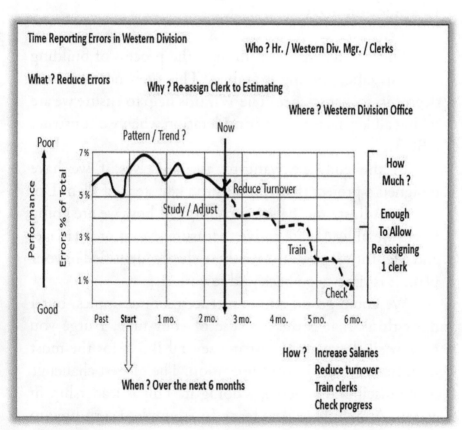

Figure 52 gives us both the plan and a way to keep on track, and figure 53 shows us the actual results. Both types should be used to keep all the participants informed of the project plans and emerging outcomes.

These BOTs are easy to construct and powerful in communicating progress and results. These are critical tools on our journey to ever better learning, accountability, and performance.

Chapter Summary

This chapter took us through the process of building some specific working examples. This does not require a degree in rocket science. The Wizards help to ensure we are taking all key factors into consideration when we construct a BOT.

In the end, we want to ask ourselves if we have designed a project that contains the key steps of Plan, Do, Check, Adjust, and have we considered how we are going to ensure all 4 Ms are active (Measure, Monitor, Manage, and Mentor). If you can't see these clearly identified in your plan, it is time to go back and rework it.

We could go on and construct more examples, but I don't think that is the best use of your time. I urge you to now sit down and construct several BOTs for the most important drivers in your operation. The biggest challenge is the discipline of actually doing it. This is leadership in action. Authentic leaders teach by example. Learn how to do it, be accountable to actually do it, experience the performance that comes with applied discipline, and show others by your example.

CHAPTER 10

CHECK: 7) Learning

Chapter Summary

This chapter expands on C of the **PDCA** cycle. If there is no time or process to check for learning, there will be no real effective learning and, thus, no change in personal or organizational capacity.

Let's reconnect on the entire eight-step process. Take a look at figure 19 shown here again. We want to set a plan in motion that has all the eight key steps embedded in a disciplined way that brings success and also builds capacity for the future. If we follow the steps with discipline, we should be successful at all three goals—learning, accountability, and performance—every time.

Figure 19

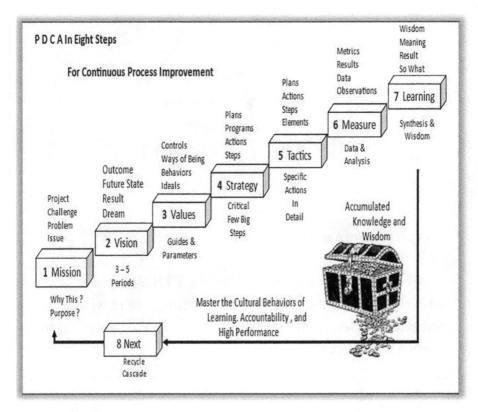

Then take another look at figure 41 shown here again. The alphabet soup acronyms we have been talking about are all shown here. While some critics might tease or be wary of all this jargon, these strings of letters/words all stand for key high-value concepts that help us to be routinely successful.

Figure 41

| PDCA, Wizards, SMARTS, 4 M, WWDWBW, MVVSTMLN Work Sheet | Name *Skinny Smith* | Start Date | *Today* | *Mission* |

P
L
A
N

P — What **S**pecific = Measure - I will : *Gain 25 pounds in 3 months by eating 5 doughnuts daily*

L — Who — *I will do this all by myself* — WWDWBW — *Vision*

A

N — Where — *In my truck, at home, at the doughnut shop, at Starbucks, etc.*

Measureable = — *Measure*

D — How — Measure = M 1 = Lag MEASURE : — *Measure and log / plot my weight every day*

O — Much — = M 1 = Lead MEASURE : — *Count and log Number of doughnuts eaten daily*

Monitor = M 2 = I will MONITOR by : *Charting / posting lead / lag data at my desk weekly*

C — Manage = M 3 = I will MANAGE by : *Share plan PUBLICLY and follow it persistently*

H — Mentor = M 4 = I will MENTOR by : *Showing others how to use the tools to be successful* — *Strategy*

E — How **A**chievable = this is within my control : *I can do this, it is just up to me; and I love doughnuts*

I will overcome the obstacles of: *Focusing on other things, & fear of the jelly filled monsters,* — *Tactics*

K — by : *doing this by noon each day* and : *smashing the jelly filled monsters before I eat them*

Why **R**elevant = drives my lag measure of: *Gain 25 pounds to make others jealous of my success* — *Values*

A

D — When **T**imed = Start : *Tuesday* with feedback check ins with : *My Manager* and *My spouse* — *Learning*

J — in *3 weeks* and *6 weeks* and in *3 months* till this becomes a habit

U — Make adjustments to the plan after each check in if needed to ensure success

S — How **S**tretch = *Practice new behavior consistently* Requiring CASA : *dedication*

T — *persistence, [and bigger pants]* for me, which I can master and use on my next project — *Next*

A full and deep understanding of each of these acronyms means we can string together the most appropriate high-value leadership behaviors that build a culture of learning, accountability, and performance. I think of them like pearls of wisdom worth memorizing and then using routinely. Each pearl seems quite simple, familiar, and relatively unimportant till they are linked into this high-value eight-step process. It is the system of steps, the template, that makes each one important.

You certainly would not need to use all these. But knowledge of them and the value they bring in ensuring we have a good PLAN make them valuable to know. You will likely have one or two favorites. After years of working in the area of managing large groups and projects, I tend to just think **PDCA**. I go looking for these four key steps. And these simple acronyms help me ensure I have a good handle on all the important aspects of the work at the start. Think CASA!

When it comes to learning, we need to stop and take stock of what we PLANned, what we did, what we got, and how we can do better next time. This seems so simple. Broken **PDCA** cycles due to lack of leader discipline mean we keep reinventing the wheel.

This is where authentic leadership behaviors really stand out. If the leader fails to ensure there is a check cycle, there won't be one. If the leader fails to make participants comfortable that this is not a witch hunt for blame, the most important facts will not emerge. If the leader fails to set the tone for learning, no learning will occur.

A leader may want to follow a pattern of inquiry that shows others that the learning process in step 7 is safe, fun, and effective. If you were about to enter a meeting where your boss and teammates were going to review a project and some of your work would fall prey to criticism, what would you hope your leader would do? How would they set the stage for a review? How would they set up the review process to ensure this time was well spent finding ways to improve rather than just finding someone to pin the problems on? When you are in charge, you need to be sure you set the cultural tone for learning, accountability, and performance.

You would want to know that this time would be used as a learning opportunity. You would want to know everyone would be working to make this a chance to improve the overall process. You would be hopeful for understanding and forgiving peers and leadership. You would want everyone to focus on the overall process, not bore down on individual actors.

If you are in charge of this step, what would you actually do? How would you structure the check part of the cycle in the After-Action Review (AAR) to ensure the time was well spent? You would want to assemble the key stakeholders, and then waltz around the **PDCA** circle again. You would want your review group to carefully and thoughtfully revisit each stage of the eight-step process.

1) What was the **Mission**?
2) What was the **Vision**?
3) What were the **Values**?
4) What was the **Strategy**?
5) What were the **Tactics**?
6) What were the **Measures**?
7) What did we **Learn**?
8) What are we going to do **Next**?

M V V S T M L N

The eight steps are the road map for success and the road map for reviewing a project. At each point, take the time to reflect as a group on what we thought we were going to do and what we actually did. As expected, we likely made changes along the way. Did we go back and document those to update the eight steps? Were we able to march through the steps with discipline and dignity? Were we, individually and as a group, able to honor and operate with respect for the initial stated values? If we did have hiccups or upsets, were we able to manage those culturally so each and every person felt included, valued, worthy of our respect, and happy to consider working with us next time?

The US military has embraced the use of tools like AAR in a big way going back many decades. Of all the organizations on the planet in the history of the world, can you think of any organization that has studied and dedicated more resources to be the best they can be?

They know and teach that smart leaders find a way to embed learning processes in the workflow. They challenge their organization to make learning as important as producing since continuous hands-on learning with real-world timely situations creates sustainable capacity to produce at higher levels at each succeeding stage. I encourage you to study AAR. I recommend the document outlining how the army uses AAR, which is the book *From Post-Mortem to Living Practice: An In-depth Study of the Evolution of the After-Action Review* by Marilyn J. Darling and Charles S. Parry.

Figure 54 offers some planning guidance for conducting an effective AAR.

Figure 54

After Action Review Planning Framework

These can be formal high level , informal, and even personal .. The steps are essentially the same

Ensure key stakeholders know this will occur from the time the project begins

These can be at the very end of a project , or even at key midpoints

1. Hold the review as soon as possible, mid project and after the work is complete
2. Include the key stakeholders including customers of our output
3. Invites and detailed agenda sent well in advance so have time to think about it
4. Create a learning atmosphere– PDCA not PDCB
5. Empower a non involved facilitator that engages everyone equally
6. Revisit the eight steps – separately, slowly, and carefully

   MV V ST M L N

6. For each step ask : [seek root causes = 5 Why's?]

   What went well? , How and Why?

   What could have gone better ? , How and Why?

   What did we learn ? How and Why?

   What should we start , continue, or stop doing ?

7. Document and implement the learnings

   Ensure learnings are now embedded in our processes

Figure 55 offers some guidance about how much time to expect to need for each phase. This is only intended to be useful for a newcomer. Once you are under way, you will need to adjust to ensure a good review, no matter how much time it takes.

Figure 55

Key Steps in an AAR Process

Foundation— a spirit of openness and learning
Focus only on things within our direct influence or control
Seek and develop multiple views

25% What were we trying to do ?	Mission, Vision, Values , Strategy
25% What did we actually do ?	Tactics , Measures
25% What did we learn ?	Learning
25% What are we going to do next ?	Next

Figure 56 offers some useful example questions.

Figure 56

After Action Review Questions

Some Useful Questions
Ensure everyone speaks their mind!

What went well ?

Why certain actions were taken ?

What could have gone better ?

How well we reacted to emerging situations?

What alternatives were available at that time ? Were there better choices?

What is not being said so far ?

What question , if asked, would help us understand this better ?

What fears were acting in the group that may have contributed to what we actually did ?

What did I/you/we do well that I/you/
we need to keep doing? What do I/
you/we need to do better next time?
—*Adam Kahane*

The focus is not on what we did wrong since there is little chance that we will get to actually repeat this exact exercise again. The issue is what can I/you/we do to improve our capacity going forward.

Our similarities make us strong, and
our differences make us even stronger.

Sometimes there will be disagreements on how these critical questions get answered. While some might view this as detrimental, the opposite is true. This is the very opportunity we have been looking for to demonstrate our learning and skill as authentic leaders. The more we can talk about our differences, the more we are likely to be able to resolve them.

Strength lies in differences,
not in similarities.
—*Stephen Covey*

Conflict averse individuals make poor leaders in the pursuit of facts in such situations. They tend to just want everyone to get along. The same weakness drives poorly constructed initial plans and then later plan reviews. Authentic leaders know the group needs to mature in its ability to tell the truth as they see it. Clearly, tact and sensitivity are needed. Group growth in capacity is waiting on the other side of airing conflicts if it is done well.

Some leaders want to just ignore or gloss over the emerging conflicts in a project review. Being polite is one thing. Ignoring the very facts that lead to organizational learning, accountability, and performance is quite another. Many are afraid of the hurt feelings when damaging facts emerge. Clearly if not done well, future collaboration will be more difficult. Be sure you are using measured facts, not opinions, to drive improvement.

Authentic leaders, arise; your big challenge awaits. Here is the opportunity to show what you are made of. Do you have the skill and the will to take on the tough role of leader? There are many good books on this subject. I recommend *Fierce Conversations: Achieving Success at Work and in Life* by Susan Scott and *The Power of Appreciative Inquiry: A Guide to Positive Change* by Diana Whitney and Amanda Trosten-Bloom.

For me, the biggest takeaway from all this is we each need to face reality. Things rarely ever go perfectly. They don't. If we tell everyone before we ever start a project that we will be reviewing it carefully, after then, they will be expecting it. If I as a leader lead the process with tact and sensitivity, I will gradually show them by example of my behavior that we are here to learn, not punish. My behavior during these reviews will drive the outcome now and the culture going forward.

We want to face facts. The more facts we have, the more likely we will be making higher-quality decisions. Everyone on our team needs to be in pursuit of our collective MVVSTMLN.

Chapter Summary

By time we get here, all the hard work is done. We either were successful with the project and our learning or we weren't.

> *The big question is what are*
> *we going to do next?*
> *How will we, and the*
> *future, be different?*

CHAPTER 11

ADJUST: 8) Next

Chapter Summary

This chapter briefly recaps the thinking behind the eight-step process now that you have worked your way through all the details. You've come this far; the rest of your journey awaits.

I won't take you back to the eight steps again. By now you either have decided to try this or you still have reservations. It either resonates with you and looks useful, or it looks too complicated to master or too time-consuming. Only you can make that decision.

Think about how you felt when you learned to ride a bike or create your first Excel spreadsheet. Don't let the newness keep you from improving your ability to learn. Even if you never use some of the eight steps, just knowing there is a logical disciplined path to higher levels of learning, accountability, and performance should be useful.

*If you think learning is expensive, try
estimating the cost of ignorance.*
—Howard Gardner

For all of us as leaders, the burning question is always what to do next. That is the inflection point where our future lies. We never have enough good information to make a perfect PLAN, and we always find out as we go along that we need to change our PLANS. Ahhhh, learning! The big question for me is are we actually aware of that process, the thinking behind our actions?

*For years I had been the greyhound
chasing the rabbit of permanent
solutions here at Smith & Hawken.
If I worked just a little harder, a
little longer, a little more creatively,
I would eventually catch the rabbit.
I would experience commercial
nirvana, and our business—
importing and marketing quality
garden tools—would run perfectly.
But I was wrong. In business you will
always have problems. They are where
the opportunities lie. A problem is an
opportunity in drag: a mess is a pile of
opportunities in drag. A good business
has interesting problems; a bad business*

has boring ones. Good management
is the art of making problems so
interesting and their solutions so
constructive that everyone wants to
get to work and deal with them.
—Paul Hawken, Growing a Business

My goal in writing this book is to help people discover the value of disciplined systems thinking and action, leading to better outcomes. I hope this works for you.

If you made it this far and you still have questions, you can always write to me at hwimmer@pacbell.net, and I will try to help you on your journey!

Good Luck!

CHAPTER 12

———— ✺ ————

Let's Talk About Systems Thinking (ST)

Chapter Summary

This is the supplementary chapter on systems thinking that I promised in the preface. I think systems thinking (ST) skills are critical to be an effective leader. I wanted this book to be about the eight-step template. I did not want to complicate understanding of that by introducing this first. But I do hope you digest, enjoy, and find this useful. And if you chose to read this first, I think you will find the rest of the book easier to digest and more valuable for having done so.

I have been studying ST for over thirty years. The only reason I am qualified to talk about systems thinking is that I have been the victim and perpetrator of a lot of systems.

I am certainly no expert. I have collected information, read many books, and attended many sessions, learning about it from the experts in the field. The ideas shared here are the best ideas I have gathered from them over that long period of time. These are not my original thoughts; they are an amalgam of what I think is best to know about ST in wording that you can easily use.

A lot of this wording can be found in the texts I have referenced, changed by my own interpretations and examples. I encourage you to check out the books *Learning Organizations* by Fred Kofman et al. for a good start, *Systems Thinking Basics: From Concepts to Causal Loops* by Virginia Anderson and Lauren Johnson, and finally, *Thinking in Systems* by Donella Meadows.

Systems are all around us. You have systems for paying your bills, keeping food in the house, maintaining your home and vehicles, maintaining your weight, remembering birthdays, brushing your teeth, the HVAC system that keeps you comfortable, the irrigation system in your yard, etc. Most of them are there doing their job, yet are undocumented and unappreciated. The question is, do we ever think of the systems that we rely on?

Before we go any further, just to give you a sample of ST in action, I want to share one example for your consideration. This is the best simple example I have ever heard. I picked it up along the way, but unfortunately, do not know who to credit for it. Suppose a fire breaks out in your town. What if this is your house? This is an <u>event.</u> If you respond by putting out the fire, you're reacting (that is, you've done nothing to prevent new fires).

If you respond by extinguishing the fire and then studying where fires occur, you would be paying attention to <u>patterns</u> of events. You might notice that fires occur in certain areas of town and move to buy a new fire truck or install a new fire station. You would be adapting and coping, but you still haven't done anything to prevent new fires.

Now suppose you look at the deeper systems involved in fire situations such as smoke detectors, fire suppression systems, building material flammability, and types of heat sources involved in the ignition of fires. Next, you upgrade building codes to incorporate what you've learned. Now you are changing the housing system to prevent fires.

You might say you are looking "upstream" of the event to intervene. Check out the book *Upstream: The Quest to Solve Problems before They Happen* by Dan Heath. Of course, this does little to fix existing houses unless you conduct a campaign about home fire prevention that installs smoke detectors, installs sprinklers, clears away flammable storage, and creates fire safe distances between structures. This looking for leverage points upstream to change the outcomes you are getting is the essence of systems thinking.

At work, you have systems to plan and do all kinds of things that need doing: budgeting, payroll, accounts payable, product delivery, reviewing contracts, managing projects, etc. Some of them are formal, and most are just informal. Whether we acknowledge it or not, they are systems just the same. We need to know more about the systems we rely on in order to effectively build and lead organizations to success.

> *The absence of a system may*
> *be your way of coping,*
> *and yes, that is in itself a system, isn't it?*

The fact that your systems may not be written down is unimportant. Certain proven patterns of behavior need to be followed, or things go haywire. Think of all the little nuances of how you keep track and manage to pay your bills. It would take a number of passes to teach all this, with all the nitty-gritty details, to someone else. For you it is easy to use since you built the system, even though it is not likely documented. This system was created in your brain and now is embedded in your behaviors.

Most of us haven't spent any time studying the process of how systems form and work. Systems are really and simply just the way things work or don't. Like you, I have been the victim and perpetrator of many systems. It wasn't till I started studying this more that I discovered there is a whole world of information and informed thinking that can make us smarter in how we build and operate the systems we use to survive and thrive.

ST offers you a powerful new *perspective*, a *vocabulary*, and a *set of tools* that you can use to better understand and address stubborn recurring problems in your everyday work and life. ST is a way of understanding reality that primarily emphasizes the relationships between a system's parts, in addition to the parts themselves. Based on a field of study known as systems dynamics, ST has practical every day application that rests on a solid theoretical foundation.

Why is ST important? ST can help you co-create smart, enduring solutions to everyday problems. In its simplest sense, ST gives you a more complete picture of reality so you can work with a system's natural forces, including human energy, to achieve the results you seek.

ST also encourages you to think about problems and solutions with an eye toward both the short and the long view. For example, how might a particular change you are considering improve your system today and play out over the long term? What unintended consequences might it have? Finally, ST is founded on some basic universal principles/patterns that you will begin to detect in all aspects of life once you learn to look for and recognize them.

What exactly is a system? A system is a group of interacting, interrelated, and interdependent parts (frequently actions) that form a complex and unified whole. Systems are everywhere. Some examples are the HR Department in every organization, the circulatory system in our bodies, the predator-prey relationships in nature, the ignition system in our cars, and the parking system where you work.

Ecological systems and human systems are "living" systems; man-made systems such as cars and washing machines are "nonliving" systems. Wise systems thinkers focus most attention on living systems, especially the human side of systems. Let's face it, organizations without the humans would produce nothing.

Process, engineering, and design specialists tend to focus more on nonliving systems. Increasingly, we are called upon to consider how the human side of systems affect the larger ecological systems of our planet, thus, our lives and the lives of future generations.

A system can be described as having the following features:

1) <u>Fits within and supports a larger system</u>. The electrical system in a car exists to serve the purposes of

the larger vehicle. It goes with the car and exists to serve the car. University organizations exist to serve the larger university, not the opposite. Company HR departments exist to serve the company, not the opposite.

2) <u>All of the system's parts must be present</u> for the system to carry out its purpose optimally. Organization systems consist of people, equipment, and processes. If you removed any one of these elements, the system could no longer function properly. It would not be a complete system.

3) <u>The parts must be arranged in a specific way</u> for the system to carry out its purpose optimally. If you rearranged reporting relationships in your department so that the experienced head of the department reported to the newest entry-level person, the department would likely have a harder time carrying out its mission effectively.

4) <u>Systems change in response to feedback</u>. The concept of feedback plays a central role in ST. Feedback is information that returns to its source and influences subsequent actions. For example, if you turn too sharply while rounding a curve in the road, visual cues (that infernal mailbox) loom into view and remind you that you are turning too sharply. Given this feedback, you jerk back to a safer course and save the mailbox—feedback in action!

5) <u>Systems maintain their stability by making adjustments based on feedback</u>. Example: Your body maintains its weight by balancing your metabolic needs. If you get too warm or too cold, your internal systems react to bring you back to that range.

Please take a look at figure 57. Here are some more examples of feedback. There are basically two kinds. Reinforcing feedback means you steadily get more and more of something unless you act to balance it by some intervening action. Things keep getting better and better or worse and worse. Balancing feedback means change has internal forces that balance it, so growth is always being offset by counteracting forces.

Systems are normally made up of both reinforcing and balancing forces. Think of hunger, eating, and your weight. You can stop the hunger by eating. No problem. But then guilt and tight clothing begin to appear, and then you perhaps make corrections. This demonstrates reinforcing and balancing loops in action.

ST has been described as having three main aspects: *perspective* (a way of looking at things); *vocabulary* (a way to describe what we see); and *tools* (a way to analyze and intervene with what we see). As for *perspective*, think: Events, Patterns of Events, and Systems.

As for *perspective*, ST helps us to see the events and patterns in our lives in a new light and respond to them in new, more enlightened systemic ways.

Figure 57

Examples of Feedback in Systems Thinking

Reinforcing Feedback Examples	Balancing Feedback Examples
Team Morale	HVAC Thermostat
Paranoia	Food and population balance
Amplifier feedback squeal	Car cruise control
Population growth	Body temperature
Credit card debt if unpaid	Hunger / thirst
Rumors	Predator and prey populations
Epidemics of disease	Leadership
Nuclear reactions	Driving a car
Savings account interest	Breathing
Chain letters	Elections
Panic attacks	Selling
Self confidence	Elections

ST has its own *vocabulary*. This improves our ability to have effective dialogues about:

a) The "whole," rather than the parts, stressing the role of interconnection, including the very important role we humans each play in the systems at work in our lives. This is the human side of the system.

b) The critical need for feedback (for example, A leads to B, which leads to C, which leads back to A) rather than the more common linear cause-and-effect thinking (A leads to B, which leads to C, which leads to D, and never comes back to A), etc. This lack of feedback and checking leads to Band-Aid fixes that then reemerge again later over and over rather than systemic fixes.

c) How systems flow and behave, including reinforcing forces (which build and build) and balancing forces (feedback that returns things to stability, limiting change).

Systems Thinking as a *set of tools*
The field of ST has generated a broad array of tools that let you

1. graphically map your understanding of a systems structure and behavior,
2. communicate with others using the map about your understanding, and
3. design high-leverage interventions for poor system performance.

These tools include

a) Causal Loop Diagrams,
b) Behavior Over Time Graphs,
c) Connection Circles,
d) Stock and Flow Diagrams, and
e) Systems Archetypes.

While it may seem a bit elementary, for starters, I highly recommend *The Shape of Change* by Rob Quaden and Alan Ticotsky for a better understanding of these tools. I found it very useful.

You can also look these up on the internet. They are pretty easy to digest and learn. They all look at the system in question in different ways. They all promote shared understanding and effective intervention. At the most sophisticated level, fancy and expensive "flight simulators" help you test the potential impact of proposed interventions.

The ones I list above are usually free and easy to obtain, learn, and use. I encourage you to study these to go deeper. At a minimum, I recommend you fully understand how to make and use Behavior Over Time Graphs (BOTs). You can learn about BOTs easily on the internet. There are many types and examples on YouTube. We will do some BOT charting elsewhere in the chapter on measurement.

Whether you consider ST mostly a new perspective, a vocabulary, or a set of tools depends on your level of experience with the subject. ST has a power and a potential that, once you've been introduced, is hard to resist. The more you learn about this intriguing field, the more you will want to know! I urge you to look into this; it may be the most promising field of study, thinking, and being you will ever encounter. It was for me.

Think of how you tie your shoes. You have an unwritten system for this that has become so rote that you can do it in the dark without looking. It is a system just the same. Try some small change in that pattern of motions today, perhaps starting with the first loop on the other side, and see if you are still proficient. We do things in the same way each time for efficiency. We do things differently periodically when we are trying to learn better ways.

When something goes wrong, we look for the cause in the hopes of making a speedy recovery to get back to what we were trying to do in the first place. We blame the systems we rely on, like the accounting system, the transportation system, the HVAC system, the plumbing system, the internet, etc. We are the creators of these systems. They usually, but not always, serve the intended purpose.

> *With a new systems trial, we sometimes*
> *get the intended consequence, and*
> *unfortunately, we always get all of*
> *the unintended consequences.*
> *—Unknown*

When things go haywire, a common reaction is the creation of yet another overlaying system to ensure this specific failure does not happen to us again. Most times, this is like putting a Band-Aid on top of prior Band-Aids.

A more important question is what was the root cause of the failure in the first place? If we can fix that, then perhaps the secondary effects will be avoided, and we won't need a second overlaying system. How much of the work an organization does falls into this category; work-arounds and system fixes? We will talk more about root cause in the core of the book.

Think of what you hear when listening to the news about some tragic incident. The newscaster, talking head, or the politician explains what is being done so this "will never happen again." Then ask yourself if what they are proposing is dealing with the fundamental issue or only the secondary effects. Are they going to prevent fires or just put out fires in the future?

Do you think they are dealing with the core issue and root cause? Once you begin to listen this way, you will be moving toward being a more capable systems thinker.

> *Every system is perfectly designed*
> *to get the result that it does.*
> *—W. Edwards Deming*

Systems contain both physical elements and the relationships between the elements in a web that join to meet the challenge. We tend to think of systems in terms of their physical parts since they are tangible—easy to see, talk about, and manipulate.

Imagine your car going down the road. The engine, transmission, and brakes all need to be working well with each other in order to proceed safely. You are usually very unaware of this complex system at your disposal. Each part can be doing its job perfectly, but if they don't work in concert, you may be sitting idle at the roadside.

I recall someone at a ST conference asking if a car without a steering wheel was still a car. Her contention was it was no longer a car since as a system, it could no longer perform the functions of a car; it was just a pile of parts. Interesting!

A huge part of system effectiveness is the smooth relationship between the parts. You can't put the brakes of a VW Bug on a semitruck and expect good outcomes. That is the essence of the science of ST for inanimate objects. In most systems, both formal (documented with process steps and rules, etc.) and informal (we just do what we always did with no formal documentation), we, the humans, rely on our use of the physical system elements to get our work done.

Yet nothing really happens until the humans show up. Pumps, HVAC units, vehicles, accounting data inputs or reports, etc., are all dependent on some human guidance or intervention to be designed and built in the first place and then to be relied on for useful outcomes.

The usefulness and productivity of each system has a physical side and a human side. The physical side is there and easy to see, and the human side is usually largely unseen except in observed behaviors. We rarely talk effectively about the human side since it is largely unseen, extremely complex, and thus much harder to define and agree on. It is easiest to just avoid this mess. We go on talking about the physical elements of the system as if they are the source of our issues, usually avoiding the human side—the most critical side of the system.

Physical components do not have good days or bad days. They do not have attitudes, grudges, faulty opinions, or learning disabilities. They do not get headaches or the flu. They do not choose to work or not work. Unless they are broken, worn out, or defective, they do what they were designed to do and are programmed, every time, the same way. They stand at the ready and perform when the humans give direction.

Humans, by comparison, have attitudes, fears, in-law troubles, appreciations, hopes, intentions, wants, jealousies, urges, feelings, doubts, aches and pains, memories of former injustices, long-held and unrecognized or secret biases, uncertainties, desires, on and on. Each of us shows up with all this baggage either promoting or detracting from our ability to cooperate and perform. Machines do not choose to give or withhold support or discretionary effort. Humans do constantly, based on how they feel.

When we talk about personal and organizational performance, we are talking about our lives in a deep, wide, incomprehensible ocean of systems, systems made up of both the physical and human sides. And how we are feeling when we show up affects the work we do, affects all the people around us, indeed the entire organization.

As supervisors and managers, we are in search of ways to improve learning, accountability, and performance. In order to do this, we need to maintain a clear and effective intense focus on the largely unseen human side of the system.

> *When we talk about systems, we tend*
> *to focus on the physical elements*
> *while the powerful levers of*
> *performance are the human*
> *side of the system.*

This is much harder than it sounds since it means that instead of just working in and on the world of inanimate objects, we have to work in and on the system of human capacities and foibles, which are fraught with all that messy stuff like bias, fuzzy thinking, clarity, envy, anger, frustration, unjustified certainty, and motivation. We humans withhold or provide cooperation and support based on our level of motivation.

For the subject of motivation, let's talk about the discretionary effort of the humans, the prime mover in most systems. We each choose to bring our full energy, creativity, and output to a task or we don't. We make constant decisions to go full on, to full off, and everywhere in between with each challenge we face. That decision lies deep within us and affects everything we do every day. Usually we are not even fully aware of those decisions.

We can apply or withhold our discretionary effort easily. Understanding this will help you fully understand the power of this factor in human relationships, the human side of the system, and output.

> *Discretionary effort is the level*
> *of effort people could give if they*
> *wanted to, but above and beyond*
> *the minimum required.*
> *—Aubrey C. Daniels, PhD*

In this modern computer-driven information age, except in the most physical of tasks, others would have a hard time knowing if we are fully applying ourselves to any assigned task. It is very, very easy to delay, waste time, create roadblocks, and then give excuses as to why some tasks are taking too long. Unfortunately, it is very easy to be a subtle saboteur of most processes if you want to. It may even be less than intentional on your part, emerging out of your subconscious mind, due to some deep, unrecognized feeling.

For example, in some office work requiring you to collaborate with others, say on the phone, you can easily report you were unable to reach that person. Or you are waiting for replies, or some missing some minor detail, or some other lame excuse that sounds plausible. "We ran out of printer paper," "My dog ate my homework," "My alarm clock broke," etc.

You may have chosen to spend some time cruising the internet looking for car insurance deals or talking on the phone to your aunt Sally. No one would know, especially now, when a lot of work is done remotely, and everyone is on the internet all day anyway. Who gets to decide what is real work and what just looks like work if it were to be observed? Internal motivation to be accountable and stay focused to produce has never been more critical.

As for motivation, it comes from within. It is meaningless to say we are going to motivate someone else. Study the literature on motivation; it will improve your understanding and ability to work well with and lead others. Other than the fear of physical force, we each individually and in real time choose if, how, and when we will fully cooperate and fully apply our best talents and energy.

Think WIIFM (What's In It For Me?). I will bring my full discretionary effort when I think it is the best thing for me to do. The best you as the leader can do is create the conditions under which I will choose to bring my best efforts.

Now by me introducing WIIFM, you may be thinking that I am suggesting this is all about pay. "Pay me more, and I will do more." You would be mistaken. I think the literature is quite clear. With some obvious exceptions, most people just want to be treated fairly. Most are not actually driven by money, unless they are financially needy. They do want to have a say in what they will be doing and how to do it. People want agency. Go look that up! Human agency is defined as an individual's capacity to determine and make meaning from their environment through purposive consciousness and reflective and creative action.

People want to be inspired by their leaders and an inspiring mission for the organization and its vision of the future. They want to be acknowledged for their efforts. This is the natural drive for agency and self-governance. Most of us want to "want to," except where there are cultural obstacles that dampen or inhibit that drive to give our best efforts. It is the role of the leader to create the conditions under which people feel fully motivated. I believe people really do want to work hard and contribute. They are just waiting to be inspired and liberated from fear and uninspiring obstacles.

There is a huge difference in organizational output between "have to" and "want to." Many studies have shown this going back decades. Some studies suggest the difference is as much as 300 percent. That is to say, a person who feels like they "have to" do something would have a certain output. If they could be internally inspired and motivated for some reason, they could then produce as much as three times that output.

Ya gotta wanna!

That sounds like wild exaggeration. Yet if you think about it in your own life, say doing yard work, you might come to realize that some days you dawdle along, enjoying the fresh air and sunshine, and other times you are motivated to get done early so you can go fishing or play golf, where you could care for the same yard in half or even one-third of the time with the same quality.

Think of riding a bike. You can ride along at a slow comfortable pace, or you can press yourself and, with some effort, go three times as fast. An observer can see the bike and your speed, but they cannot see your motivation. You do this all the time in everything you do. Same bike, same road, same person, just more discretionary effort. You make a conscious choice to fully apply yourself or to take your sweet time. Most casual observers could not tell the difference in motivation, yet the differences can be large in terms of individual or collective productivity.

Figure 58 shows the concept of how discretionary effort can boost individual and collective performance. If people are inspired by the mission, vision, values, strategy, and the behaviors of their leaders, high levels of individual and collective performance are possible. This comes from a strong focus on getting the right results the right way.

Figure 58

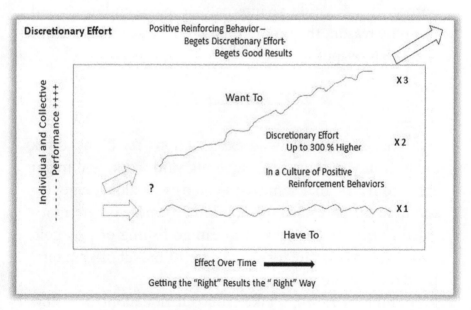

What if 300 percent improvement just sounds too outrageous? What if you or your organization could just be steadily 30 percent more effective? What if you have a hard time buying the idea of even 30 percent? What if the difference was only 3 percent?

What if you or your organization was just steadily and persistently 3 percent more effective all the time, every time, over time? You know about compound interest. And if you don't, you need to go look it up. What if your organization was steadily and persistently just 3 percent better than your competition? Or what if productivity was just 3 percent higher every day, all year? Just 3 percent steadily compounded can have huge effects on you and/or your organization's success.

You would gradually bury your competition. Steady yet minor changes in discretionary effort by an individual or an organization make huge differences in accumulated output and thus success over time. Few leaders ever really think about how such a small difference would add up when applied to perhaps tens or hundreds of people. This may be an inspiring mental model for you to explore.

One time years ago, I figured out how much this might affect output in the service organization I was leading. At that time, our organization had about three hundred people. If each person decided to just waste an extra fifteen minutes every day (less than two minutes an hour) beyond the normal level of unnoticed and uncontrollable wasted time, all at once or scattered in little drips through the day, just chatting, doing personal errands on the phone, or dawdling and talking instead of being focused on their work, it would matter big time!

I bet you can waste that much time without even thinking about it. What would the collective effect on output be? That fifteen minutes would be a 3 percent loss in productivity, the equivalent of another nine workers in a three-hundred-person organization. Think of how organizations struggle to justify adding just a few people or laying a few people off.

The motivation to be focused really matters. Small persistent habitual leaks of time can continually drag the organization down. Motivation to stay focused on the work has big payouts. But remember, we cannot force inspiration. What if our people were so excited to be working together on this project they did not want to go home? That if their coffee cup was emblazoned with "thank God it's Monday!"

Do the math for your own situation. What if your organization's mission, vision, values, and strategy and leaders' behaviors were so inspiring, everyone just wanted to give all their discretionary effort and work at a high level of output all the time? The effect would be huge.

The culture, driven mostly by persistently motivating leadership behaviors, can make huge differences in learning, accountability, and performance. This is the leverage the human side of the system can provide, but only when we acknowledge it and work to improve.

The median US male makes about $65,000 per year in 2022. Organizations have to pay another about $35,000 per year for benefits, etc. So the added nine people would cost the organization $900,000 per year to make up for the unnoticed wasted time. What if instead of wasting the less than two minutes each hour, the employees were so inspired, they actually worked harder to the tune of two minutes more productive above the normal waste of time? Do you think that is possible? I do. I think under the right conditions, they could easily be much more effective than that.

Taken a bit further, we can apply this to the differences between individuals. Let's say person one is a typical average worker. They come to work on time and stay till quitting time, do what is necessary with adequate quality, don't make many errors, don't waste too much time, and get along with others. They are the middle ground of performance. Every organization needs people like this. They are the heart and soul of most organizations. This describes the huge middle segment of every workforce.

Person two might be more inspired and thus motivated to arrive and start every day just a bit early, say, just two minutes before and after starting time, break time, lunchtime, afternoon break, and at the end of the day. They always do more than what was expected. They rarely make errors, and when they do, the issue is quickly reported and corrected by them with lots of apologies. They take accountability willingly.

They not only get along; they are the ones others come to for help and guidance. These are our star performers. These are the ones who usually get promoted and become the organization's leaders while most of the average performers remain puzzled why others were chosen. The differences are small but persistent and very important for both personal and organizational success.

What about the other end of the spectrum? Another person finds no inspiration here for some reason. They are a poor fit for this work, or they are stuck by some obstacle, personally or in the organization. They are always slow to start, early to finish, and take their sweet time in every action in between. This could easily lead to lower personal and of course organizational productivity. More, these folks are the ones supervisors and managers spend the most time with. Coaching, documenting, working with HR for some way to move this person out consumes a lot of time.

Unfortunately, we know supervisors and managers spend an inordinate amount of time fiddling with poor performers at the expense of the others and the organization. They could better use this time creating the conditions leading to high motivation. Failing to deal effectively with this in a timely way drags down the whole enterprise. This is weak leadership in action.

So how do we create the conditions where others feel motivated to give their discretionary effort? We work to create the conditions under which they see themselves aligned with the mission, vision, values, and strategy of the organization. They need to feel that their best interests will be served by bringing their discretionary effort to fully bear on the work at hand. WIIFM? There are many, many sources of information on this. In my experience, the best ideas come from work in the Applied Behavioral Sciences.

The Applied Behavioral Sciences focus on how to provide meaningful positive reinforcement feedback to those performing tasks. I urge you to look up "positive reinforcement" on the internet now. That will help you to more fully appreciate the immense value of knowing how and when to give positive reinforcement feedback (feedback is the most critical element of ST) that builds the kind of relationships and cultures we seek.

We humans need quality feedback to produce sustained high outcomes for learning, accountability, and high performance in individuals and the organization. I encourage you to study more about this. I recommend *Fierce Conversations: Achieving Success at Work and in Live* by Susan Scott and *The Power of Appreciative Inquiry: A Practical Guide to Positive Change* by Diana Whitney and Amanda Trosten-Bloom.

> ### *We live in the organizational cultures we build, tolerate, and thus deserve.*

Before we move on, I want to provide an entertaining mini exposé on brushing your teeth. Yes, that's right, you heard it here first. When you brush your teeth, you are reenacting a system, a daily system to clean and protect your dental health. Your teeth, the toothpaste, sink, and toothbrush and how they are laid out for the work are the physical elements of this system. They are the necessary base of operations for this system. But nothing really happens till the human side of the system is activated.

First, you have to "want to" brush your teeth. You have to be inspired. We are not sure just what your complex motivation is. Perhaps you can still hear your mother pressing you. Or perhaps it was your dentist at your last checkup. Perhaps it was your desire to have shiny white teeth or a great smile, or perhaps the need to repair bad breath after the salami sandwich at noon? Nevertheless, you find you are motivated to get this task done, a critical first requirement. Do you have to or do you want to? It matters in how you will actually do it.

Now, you can approach this task at full speed or a relaxed pace. The efficiency of this work is totally up to you and the discretionary effort you bring to the task. The physical elements like toothpaste and brush are important elements. Yet nothing will happen in this system till the human motivation and energy show up. Think of all the parents this morning cajoling their children to do a good job brushing their teeth before school.

It is this way with all systems. Humans use computers and machines to get work done. But it is the humans who create, guide, and use the machines. Machines don't make mistakes; humans do. Machines don't have bad attitudes. Yet in our work on systems, we usually begin our pursuit of fail points by discussing the physical elements, which are rarely to blame. Think of it, the actual output is totally controlled by the human side of the system.

Garbage in, garbage out. Who
provides the garbage?

ST is a huge complex subject. I have been an avid student for three decades and am still on a steep learning curve. You may be able to manage systems with a modest understanding of its basics. I doubt anyone could really be an inspiring leader of a high-performance organization without a working knowledge of ST application on all of its many levels. I recommend the book *The Dance of Change* by Peter Senge.

Systems thinking is a discipline for
seeing wholes. It is a framework for

*seeing interrelationships rather than
things, for seeing "patterns of change"
rather than static "snapshots."*
—*Peter Senge*

This is not a book about ST, so I will stop here and point you in a very useful direction. By now, you have lost interest or are ready to dig deeper. I recommend you check out *Systems Thinking Tools and Applications* by Daniel H. Kim. You may also want to check out *thesystemsthinker. com*. This is a source of the very best simple and useful tools for working in and on systems. The key author is Daniel Kim. There is a newsletter and articles across the spectrum of ST applications.

One of the biggest challenges is dealing with the complexity of our systems. The idea of complexity is, well, complex. Most of our systems today are quite complex. We have moved on from the industrial age, machine age, information age, to the age of computers. The physical elements of our systems are much more sophisticated and "smart" now than in prior times. Are we?

It would seem technology-fueled automation would have made life simple and easy for humans, all humans by now. It didn't, did it! Why not? Life seems to be becoming ever more complex. In the end, it is the humans who create and control our systems, and we the humans have not evolved to behave any differently in the past few hundred years parallel with the advance of technology. Let's face it, we are stuck with our basic human natures.

Certainly, human knowledge has expanded ever wider and deeper at an amazing pace. Think of all the advancements in technology and science. But knowledge is not wisdom. Think of the flow of events and what we make of them. We have our observations, perceptions, facts, information, knowledge, and then hopefully, we arrive at some useful wisdom.

If human wisdom had kept up, modern advances in accumulated knowledge and science should have made us capable of commanding nature and ourselves in a peaceful sustainable world. With such godlike powers, why have we done so little to build a truly humane world to approach utopia?

In the several years following the COVID pandemic of 2019, many millions died of it across the world. Science and technology produced marvels in terms of the extremely rapid and successful development of powerful vaccines. However, our human governance skills were inept.

Whole countries struggled with the human side of the system of getting the humans to do what science knew was best. We don't ever get to control the humans; we can only influence them. I think this again reinforces the mental model argument for leadership over managing. What role did the presence or absence of trust play in how this unfolded?

How do we influence the humans in our systems so they cooperate and collaborate to build advanced systems of human performance? Ahhhh, the human side of the system. If you like studying about such things, I again recommend the book *Upstream* with some excellent examples by Dan Heath.

I am reminded of reading about the work of UC Berkeley economics Professor William J. Baumol (RIP) back in the mid-1960s. He has written a number of good books. If you are an avid reader, you may want to check them out. Baumol surfaced the idea that the advancement of technology over the decades is built on the reality that each succeeding generation of tech hardware stands on the shoulders of the prior generation. Think of the evolution of phones, cars, air travel, online banking, medical imaging, 3D printing, and now emerging AI, etc.

The advancement of the human side of the system does not really work that way. Certainly, humans have continued to accumulate understanding of the physical world. However, there is no real advancement in basic human intelligence, wisdom, and behaviors as it relates to how we interact with others.

This is the human side of the systems we build and tolerate. Humans are not very good at learning vicariously from prior generations. Each generation learns their lessons and then passes away. Young people usually have to learn interaction skills by painful experience. Interaction wisdom comes slowly and generally has to be built over and over within in each succeeding person and generation.

Going back over the long span of time,
on the human side of our
systems, fundamentally, there is
nothing new under the sun.

Advice from elders is viewed with suspicion or worse. Humans are the same now as they have been for thousands of years. Sure, we are aided by our steady advancements in accumulated knowledge and physical technology, but we as a species hold little more wisdom than we had eons ago as it relates to how we interact in groups. Just look at the twenty-four-hour news.

Here is my interpretation of Baumol's thesis. There is a growing cleft in the trends. Relative to their power per unit of utility, technology costs continue to go steadily down as the value and use of capacity go up, while the cost of hands-on human labor continues to climb in relative terms. First, think of the ease of use and cost of early telephones compared to now. Better and better and cheaper and cheaper phones dominate our modern world. You can extend that to cars, airplanes, kitchen appliances, etc.

Now think of the relative cost of health care, food service workers, or anywhere that is not amenable to automation, anything that requires the "human touch." If we need humans to deliver the service, the cost of the human effort goes up over time compared to the cost of the smart and likely automated machine effort. I think that this means that as time passes, being effective in intervening on the human side of the system will become ever more important. Think about that as it relates to your personal theories of organization and about your strategy. Unless you can totally automate, you are tethered to the human side of the system. The question is: How much motivation exists in the human side of your system?

The human side of our systems—the final frontier!

Perhaps the best explanation of system complexity in the human realm for me comes from author Adam Kahane.

He has written a number of excellent books. I encourage you to find them and get started. I especially liked his book *Solving Tough Problems*. At this point, I will share just one key framework that I have adapted from Kahane's work that really goes a long way to understanding how to intervene in complex systems. I have used his ideas in my teaching and coaching work for years.

When considering how to proceed with any given challenge, we need to have a strategy. We need to understand how to proceed, improving the physical and human elements of the system to bring about improvement. Remember, in most systems, the physical elements are relatively fixed at any one point in time. The big levers of opportunity are usually on the human side. Sometimes the challenge is simple, involving only a few humans. And sometimes the system involves many brains.

Sometimes system interventions bring about immediate results, and sometimes there is a time delay between the system intervention and a different and/or better outcome. As an added complexity, perhaps a change at one point in the system will only bring obvious change in some remote other location in the system. Cause and effect may be separated by time and space and thus out of our view till new issues crop up.

Sometimes the challenge is a familiar one and prior patterns and solutions can be used, and sometimes the challenge is new and unprecedented, or the predicted outcomes are way off expectations. In these cases, we need to invent new approaches. Our interventions need to take into account all three levels of complexity, the number of humans involved, delay time or distance effects, and the fact that new outcomes never seen before may emerge, requiring creating brand-new solutions.

Kahane came up with a way of looking at the complexity of systems that is really helpful and creative. This seems quite complex at first, but in the end, it will be worth working your way through it. It will be helpful for developing your understanding of how to work with complex challenges.

Recall earlier I outlined three ways to be more effective in your systems work. Here they are again. Watch for these as we explore one of Kahane's frameworks for systems work:

1) Graphically depict your understanding of a system structure and behavior. (See examples of BOTs in the core of the book.)
2) Communicate with others about your understanding using graphic depictions of the system.
3) Design high-leverage interventions for addressing poor system performance.

See figure 59. This chart maps system complexity into three major levels. The world is more complex than this, but this is the best work I have ever seen that helps me consider some of the most impactful leverage points and ways of building a successful strategy for proceeding. They are shown down the left side as the three levels:

Social = People
Dynamic = Delay and Location
Generative = Patterns

The chart shows how to think about this moving from the simplest challenges on the left to the most complex challenges on the right. Simple problems can usually be addressed with management skills. The more complex the challenge, the more leadership is critical. I know it is complex, but take time anyway to study this chart carefully. Ask yourself how this might be applied to your latest system challenge.

Simple People (Social Complexity) problems can usually be managed by experts and authorities. The greater the number of people affected and involved, the more the need to involve participants and those most affected. Moving across left to right shows that one, few, many, or most people are impacted and thus need to be involved.

For the second level, simple problems of Dynamic Complexity (Delay and Location) can be solved piece by piece. In a simple problem, for example, there is essentially no delay issue, and the distance between the action and outcome is short and manageable. Thus, the outcomes are more predictable and can be anticipated. Once distance and delay are introduced, prediction of the interactions and outcomes become very complicated.

Figure 59

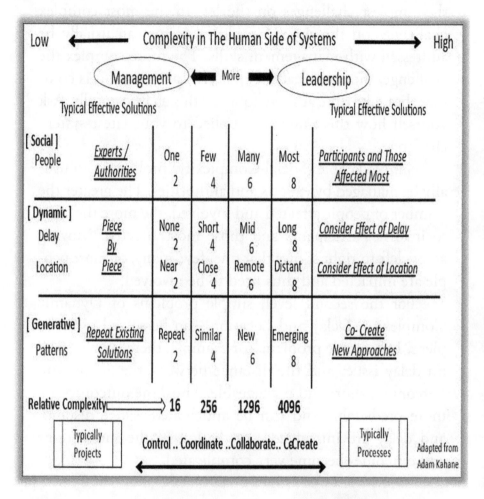

The more complex the delay and location issues, the more our strategies need to take delay and location into account. For example, as you work your way across the chart, you can see some possible gradations of delay and location, such as near, close, remote, and distant.

Where delays are long and locations are distant, we have to consider effect of delay and effect of location to a much greater extent. This actually requires us to think more in the mode of a video rather than a snapshot. We need to be able to visualize what happens as changes ripple through the system. This adds several layers of complexity to the challenge that is very hard to sort out in the short run. This is a huge driver of complexity and confusion in solving problems.

If there are delays, changes we make may not show up for a while, leaving us to believe the changes were not effective. Or worse, we might not see the effect or our change in time and abandon the change before it has the intended effect. If changes drive new outcomes in remote locations, we may miss how our good intentions drove poor outcomes in some remote place, or how our good intentions made things worse for us and better for someone at some remote location. This is a huge pit that systems thinkers have to dance around.

For the third level of complexity, we are looking at Generative Complexity (Patterns) that can be solved if we repeat existing prior solutions. The word *generative* here is related to how much creativity may be needed to generate entirely new solutions.

Think of generative as another name for old-fashioned trial and error. This is because for simple problems, we can usually rely on prior solutions, so not much creativity is required to generate a viable strategy. On complex patterns, we have to practice co-creative new approaches since this is all new territory, and prior solutions won't be effective. We have to generate a new path.

Across the bottom of the chart, the arrow shows how we must move from the arena of control to coordinating, to collaborating, to co-creating. This calls for large advances in skill and leadership behaviors. Clearly, simple problems can be solved with smart management. Complex problems need to be solved with leadership. Leaders need to harness the people and physical resources.

> *Managers discover the future;*
> *leaders make the future.*
> *—Unknown*

Embedded in the chart, there are numbers. I added these one day to help me try to understand how to better consider the effect of the degree of complexity. They are intended to be multiplied down the chart. So for the simplest challenges, you would multiply 2 for people involved, times 2 for no delay, times 2 for near location, times 2 for a repeating pattern, giving a simple problem a complexity score of 16. You might say this was the score for tying your shoes or brushing your teeth.

For the most complex problems that the world faces, like climate change or world hunger, you would multiply 8 for the fact that most people would be affected, times 8 for the long delays, times 8 for the distance between cause and effect, times 8 for the fact that there is no prior pattern or model for a solution, leading to a score of 4,096.

This would indicate an extremely complex issue is 256 times as hard to solve as a simple problem (4096/16). As shown in the boxes in the bottom corners of the chart, relatively simple problems are solved as projects while highly complex problems are solved by co-creating new processes.

Using this chart as a menu, you could consider any issue and multiply the appropriate factor going down the chart at the right level across and calculate the relative difficulty of solving any problem. Try it yourself for something you are working on. What kind of approach do you need? How does that square with this chart and the approach you are now using?

Please know this is a totally arbitrary valuing system of my own fuzzy thinking. It has not been validated by anyone, but I think it is instructional. If you have followed me this far, you will have a better mental model for understanding of the complexity of solving tough challenges.

Fortunately or unfortunately, our systems produce the results they are perfectly tuned to produce, nothing more and nothing less. If your system does not have the right parts or capacity or alignment to get what you want, you will need to fix the deficits. If you are making wadgits but want widgets, change will be needed. The changes are most likely needed on the human side of the system.

What got us here won't get us there!
—Unknown

As we move forward in the understanding of the eight-step template, we will be talking about a ST approach to learning, accountability, and performance. We will want to be focused clearly on the physical elements of our systems and even more focused on the human side or our systems.

The organizations with the
most talented leaders deepest
in the ranks wins!

—Unknown

Chapter Summary

This is the supplementary chapter on systems thinking that I promised in the preface. I think ST skills are critical to be an effective leader. I wanted this book to be about the eight-step template. I did not want to complicate understanding of that by introducing this first. But I do hope you did digest, enjoy, and find this chapter useful. And if you chose to read this first, I think you will find the rest of the book was easier to digest and more valuable for having done so.

APPENDIX A

PDCA, Wizards, SMARTS, 4 M, and MVVSTMLN Work Sheet   Name _____   Start Date _____

Mission

P   *What*   **S**pecific = Lead Measure .. I will : _____
L   *Who*   _____
A   *Where*   _____
N

Vision

Measureable = _____

Measure = M 1 = Lag MEASURE   : _____

= M 1 = Lead MEASURE : _____

Measure

D   *How*   Monitor = M 2 = I will MONITOR by : _____
O   *Much*   Manage = M 3 = I will MANAGE by : _____
             Mentor = M 4 = I will MENTOR by : _____

Strategy

C   *How*   **A**chievable = this is within my control : _____
H   I will overcome the obstacles of : _____ and : _____
E   by : _____ , _____ and : _____
C
K

Tactics

A   *Why*   **R**elevant = drives my lag measure of: _____
D   *When*   **T**imed = Start : _____   with feedback check ins with : _____   and _____

Values

J   in _____ and _____ and in _____   till this becomes a habit
U   Make adjustments to the plan after each check in if needed to ensure success

Learning

S   *How*   **S**tretch = _____ .Requiring CASA : _____
T   _____ for me, which I can master and use on my next project

Next

APPENDIX B

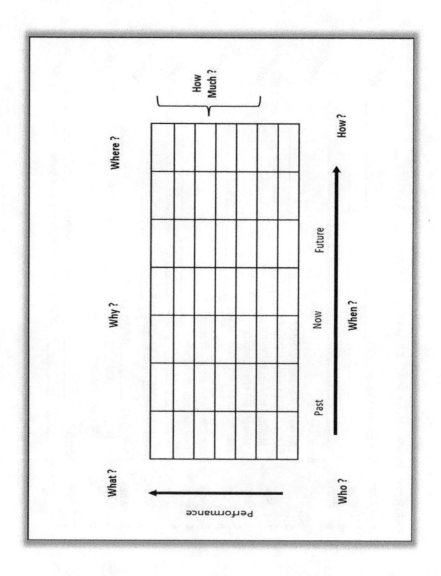

APPENDIX C

Leadership Assessment Tool ..

My Leadership Skills Are On Parade For All To See

Pg. 1

Know what to do ?

I have personally ensured that:

____ We have a truly SHARED vision of this assignment

____ We agreed on how to measure success

____ Our measures focus on the critical few issues ?

____ We stay the course– don't unfairly change objectives– during the assignment

____ They know how this work ties into our intended business results

____ They fully understand the consequences of success or failure for all of us

____ They understand latitude and limits of their responsibility and authority

Skill to do it ?

I have personally ensured that:

____ They have the technical competence (hard skills) to achieve the goal

____ They have the interpersonal skills (very hard skills) to achieve the goal

____ They understand the business risks and rewards to the organization

____ They have the skill to constructively resolve the inevitable conflicts

____ They know how the organization works– who to seek help or expertise from , etc.

____ They know how to keep meaningful metrics and act on them for success

Leadership Assessment Tool ..   Pg. 2

My Leadership Skills Are On Parade For All To See

Have the time and resources :

<u>I have personally ensured that:</u>

_____ They have the resources (time , $, support, info, equip) to be successful

_____ The processes they are supposed to follow are clear and effective

_____ That hidden fears don't restrict their discretionary effort

_____ That work is clearly prioritized and possible within the time allotted.

_____ Organizational barriers to success are dealt with

<u>Want to do it ?</u>

_____ They feel reinforced by me , and our team, as they make progress along the way

_____ They receive clear, timely, nonjudgmental, constructive feedback

_____ There are no hidden agenda's that restrict discretionary effort

_____ They know I treat everyone fairly , and hold everyone accountable for results

BIBLIOGRAPHY

Anderson, Virginia, and Lauren Johnson. *Systems Thinking Basics: From Concepts to Causal Loops.* Cambridge, Massachusetts: Pegasus Communications, 1997.

Barr, Lee, and Norma Barr, PhD. *The Leadership Equation Leadership, Management, and the Myers-Briggs.* Austin, Texas: Eakin Press, 1989.

Bossidy, Larry, and Ram Charan. *Execution: The Discipline of Getting Things Done.* New York, New York: Crown Publishing, 2002.

Brassard, Michael. *The Memory Jogger Plus +: Featuring the Seven Management and Planning Tools.* Salem, New Hampshire: GOAL/QPC, 1996.

Brown, Mark Graham. *Keeping Score: Using the Right Metrics to Drive World-Class Performance.* New York, New York: Quality Resources, 1996.

Brown, Peter, Henry L. Roediger III, Mark A. McDaniel. *Make it Stick: The Science of Successful Learning.*

Cambridge, Massachusetts: The Belknap Press of Harvard University Press, 2014.

Daniels, Aubrey C., PhD. *Bringing Out the Best in People: How to Apply the Astonishing Power of Positive Reinforcement.* New York, New York: McGraw-Hill, 2016.

Darling, Marilyn J., and Charles S. Parry. *From Post-Mortem to Living Practice: An In-Depth Study of the Evolution of the After-Action Review.* Charlestown, Massachusetts: Signet Consulting Group, 2001.

Dixon, Nancy. *The Organizational Learning Cycle: How We Can Learn Collectively.* New York, New York: McGraw Hill, 1994.

Epstein, Marc, and Bill Birchard. *Counting What Counts: Turning Corporate Accountability to Competitive Advantage.* Persues Books, 2000.

Harbour, Jerry L. *The Basics of Performance Measurement.* New York, New York: Productivity Press, 1997.

Heath, Dan. *Upstream: The Quest to Solve Problems Before They Happen.* Maryland: Avid Reader Press, 2020.

Herrmann, Ned. *The Creative Brain.* Spindale, North Carolina: The Ned Herrmann Group, 1989.

Hesselbein, Frances, Marshall Goldsmith, and Richard Beckhard. *The Organization of the Future (The Drucker*

Foundation). San Francisco, California: Jossey-Bass Publishers, 1997.

Kahane, Adam. *Solving Tough Problems: An Open Way of Talking, Listening, and Creating New Realities.* Oakland, California: Berrett-Koehler Publishers Inc., 2004.

Keirsey, David, and Marilyn Bates. *Please Understand Me: Character and Temperament Types.* Del Mar, California: Prometheus Nemesis Book Company, 1978.

Kim, Daniel H. *Systems Thinking Tools and Applications.* Pegasus Communications, 1999.

Koberg, Don and Jim Bagnall. *The Universal Traveler: A Soft-Systems Guide to: Creativity, Problem Solving, and the Process of Reaching Goals.* Los Altos, California: William Kaufmann Inc., 1972.

Kofman, Fred, Peter Senge, Rosabeth Moss Kanter, and Charles Handy. *Learning Organizations: Developing Cultures for Tomorrow's Workplace.* New York, New York: Productivity Press, 1995.

Meadows, Donella. *Thinking in Systems.* Chelsea Green Publishing, 2008.

Pfeffer Jeffrey, Robert I. Sutton. *Hard Facts, Dangerous Half-Truths, and Total Nonsense: Profiting from Evidence-Based Management.* Brighton, Massachusetts: Harvard Business Review Press, 2006.

Quaden, Alan Ticotsky and Debra Lyneis. *The Shape of Change*. Acton, Massachusetts: Creative Learning Exchange, 2004.

Scott, Susan. *Fierce Conversations: Achieving Success at Work and in Life One Conversation at a Time*. New York, New York: Berkley Publishing (Penguin Group), 2004.

Senge, Peter M. *The Fifth Discipline: The Art & Practice of The Learning Organization*. Austin, Texas: Eakin Press, 1989.

Senge, Peter M. *The Fifth Discipline Fieldbook: Strategies and Tools for Building a Learning Organization*. New York, New York: Currency Doubleday, 1994.

Senge, Peter, and George Roth. *The Dance of Change: The Challenges to Sustaining Momentum in Learning Organizations*. New York, New York: Currency Doubleday, 1999.

Tetlock, Phillip E. and Dan Gardner. *Superforecasting: The Art and Science of Prediction*. New York, New York: Penguin Random House LLC, 2015.

Whitney, Diana, and Amanda Trosten-Bloom. *The Power of Appreciative Inquiry: A Practical Guide to Positive Change*. Oakland, California: Berrett-Koehler Publishers Inc., 2003.

Printed in the USA
CPSIA information can be obtained
at www.ICGtesting.com
LVHW040740140824
788116LV00001B/198

9 798890 616333